POSTMORTEM

for

a

Postmodernist

Postmortem for a Postmodernist

Arthur Asa Berger

ALTAMIRA
PRESS

A Division of
ROWMAN & LITTLEFIELD PUBLISHERS, INC.
Walnut Creek • Lanham • New York • Oxford

ALTAMIRA PRESS
A Division of Rowman & Littlefield Publishers, Inc.
1630 North Main Street, #367
Walnut Creek, CA 94596
www.altamirapress.com

Rowman & Littlefield Publishers, Inc.
4720 Boston Way
Lanham, MD 20706

12 Hid's Copse Road
Cumnor Hill, Oxford OX2 9JJ, England

British Library Cataloguing in Publication Information Available

Library of Congress Cataloging-in-Publication Data

Berger, Arthur Asa, 1933–
    Postmortem for a postmodernist / by Arthur Asa Berger.
        p. cm.
        ISBN 0-7619-8910-2 (cloth : alk. paper).—ISBN 0-7619-8911-0 (pbk. : alk.
        paper)
        I.   Title.
    PN6727.B39P67   1997
    741.5973—dc21   97-4893
                                                                                                CIP

Printed in the United States of America

⊖™ The paper used in this publication meets the minimum requirements of
American National Standard for Information Sciences—Permanence of Paper
for Printed Library Materials, ANSI/NISO Z39.48–1992.

Interior and cover design by Denise M. Santoro
Production by Labrecque Publishing Services
Editorial management by Denise M. Santoro

table of contents

acknowl**edgments**

I would like to thank Mitch Allen, Il Supremo at AltaMira Press, for suggesting that I write a comic book on postmodernism. I decided, instead, to write a murder mystery, with lots of comic book frames that I drew (shown at the beginning of every chapter) so that I could deal with more aspects of postmodernism and do so in greater depth. I also benefited from the very detailed suggestions he provided, and the ones Denise Santoro offered, as well. I appreciate the support that Doug Kellner gave to the project. He was kind enough to look at the first draft and make some suggestions. I made great use of the marvelous book he wrote with Steven Best, *Postmodern Theory: Critical Interrogations*.

I owe enormous debts of gratitude to all the postmodern scholars whose works I have borrowed from and whom I've poked fun at in this combination satire and parody, murder mystery and comic book, and whatever else it might be.

    Postmortem for a Postmodernist is, in the best traditions of POMO, an intertextual collage. I've borrowed lines, and in some cases paragraphs, from many authors—mystery writers, philosophers, and so on. Since this is a mystery story that I've written, I won't reveal their names. I've also provided quotations from important postmodernist thinkers before each chapter, to add some verisimilitude to the book. And I've prepared a list of books on postmodernism for those who wish to explore the subject in more detail.

    I've edited a companion volume, *The Postmodern Presence: Readings on Postmodernism in American Culture and Society,* dealing with the way postmodernism has affected contemporary culture and society—mostly American, but not exclusively so.

    I hope you enjoy my murder mystery and gain a better understanding of postmodernism by reading it. Professor Ettore Gnocchi's sudden death was lamentable, but I'd like to think we all can learn a great deal from it.

author's **note**

There is a ridiculous rumor that has been widely circulated, in
letters, by phone, and on the Internet, that suggests that I did not
write this book but, instead, translated it. The book was written,
according to these rumors, by a celebrated postmodernist thinker
whose name is mentioned in this book. It has been suggested, for
example, that I translated it from French, from German, from
Italian, even from Bulgarian—languages with which I admit I have
a certain amount of familiarity and mastery. These rumors—and
let me state my position categorically—are absolutely absurd. I
wrote this book. It is an original work and not a translation. It
is a book only *I* could have written. It is a book, some would
suggest, that only I would have *wanted* to write.

pers**onae**

Ettore Gnocchi . . . the father of American postmodernism
and University Professor at the University of California at Berkeley.
Was he the kindly, lovable man he was supposed to be—or was he
a monstrous sexual predator who used his power as University
Professor to cater to his insatiable needs? He was having a dinner
party at his house with a group of colleagues who were helping
him put on a conference about postmodernism. Each person at the
dinner party had a good reason to hate Gnocchi. That might
explain why he was killed *four different ways.* But how could it be
that he was killed four ways at the same moment in time?

Shoshana TelAviv . . . Gnocchi's still-beautiful Israeli wife . . .
a postmodernist as well, and also a professor at Berkeley. Did she
know about Gnocchi's numerous liaisons, and, if she did know,
did she care? What exactly was her relationship with Gnocchi?
Was she having an affair with Alain Fess? And what was Slavomir
Propp's hand doing on her knee during the dinner party the evening that Gnocchi was murdered?

Alain Fess . . . a "brilliant" young philosopher from France who had written one important book on postmodernism. Then his career suddenly stalled. Fess wrote his dissertation under Gnocchi and barely survived the experience. There were rumors that Fess was sleeping with Shoshana TelAviv. Would it have been convenient for Fess if Gnocchi were, somehow, put out of the way?

Slavomir Propp . . . a fat Russian linguist and postmodernist, who loved to eat and had an excellent recipe for cheesecake. What was his hand doing on Shoshana TelAviv's knee at the dinner party the evening Gnocchi was murdered? Gnocchi, according to Propp, stole his ideas and published them in one of Gnocchi's most acclaimed books. Was this true? If so, why was Propp working with Gnocchi and the others to put on a conference dealing with postmodernism?

Myra Prail . . . the most recent in a long list of beautiful graduate students who were Gnocchi's research assistants. She was also doing her dissertation under his supervision. Was she working under Gnocchi in other ways? Did she have very round heels, as Miyako Fuji suggested? Or was Myra Prail a determined woman who would do anything to get ahead—and who knew exactly what she was doing?

Basil Constant . . . an English writer whose novels were considered minor classics in the postmodernist literary canon. Was he gay or bisexual? Did it matter? There were wild rumors that he was actually Thomas Pynchon. Could that be possible? What was Constant doing at Berkeley with a group of academics, since he loathed both students and professors? Did he have any designs on anyone? Myra Prail was using his novels in her dissertation; was there anything funny about that?

Miyako Fuji . . . a stylish professor of philosophy from the University of Tokyo. Ettore Gnocchi had been her dissertation advisor. She despised Gnocchi. In fact, she hated him, even though she came to America to help him put on his conference. Why was her behavior so eccentric? Why did she stare at people at times? And what was her relationship with Alain Fess? She had made a postmodernist film. How did it reflect the postmodernist sensibility? Were there such things as "postmodernism" and a postmodernist aesthetic, or was postmodernism just anything you could get away with?

Solomon Hunter . . . an enigmatic San Francisco Police Inspector. He seemed rather uninteresting, and not particularly clever. Or was that a pose? Does that explain why everyone at the dinner party was terrified of him? Or was it because nobody could figure him out, could "read" him? Hunter got an earful on postmodernism while he tried to figure out who killed Gnocchi. Did postmodernism somehow help answer the question "Who killed Ettore Gnocchi?" Does postmodernism answer any *other* questions?

It is reality itself that is hyperrealist. Surrealism's secret already was that the most banal reality could become surreal, but only in certain privileged moments that are still nevertheless connected with art and the imaginary. Today it is quotidian reality in its entirety—political, social, historical and economic—that from now on incorporates the simulating dimension of hyperrealism. We live everywhere already in an "aesthetic hallucination of reality."

Jean Baudrillard,

Simulations

(148).

chapter one

When the lights went on again,

the head of Professor Ettore Gnocchi was lying on the table. There was a small red hole, from which a thin trickle of blood was flowing, in the middle of his forehead. The handle of a silver stiletto protruded from his back, and around this stiletto the material on Gnocchi's sports jacket was stained a dark red. A long wooden dart, with yellow feathers, was lodged in his right cheek, several inches from his mouth. The glass of wine, which he had just started drinking, had spilled onto the tablecloth, from which a slightly sulfuric-smelling mist was rising.

There was, curiously, something that resembled a smile frozen on his face.

The age of resemblance is drawing to a close. It is leaving nothing behind but its games. Games whose power of enchantment grow out of the new kinship between resemblance and illusion; the chimeras of similitude loom up on all sides, but they are recognized as chimeras; it is the privileged age of *trompe-l'oeil* painting, of the comic illusion, of the play that duplicates itself by representing another play, of the *quid pro quo*, of dreams and visions; it is the age of the deceiving senses; it is the age in which the poetic dimension of language is defined by metaphor, simile, and allegory.

Michel Foucault,

The Order

of Things:

An Archaeology

of the Human

Sciences (51).

chapter two

"My God—what happened?"

screamed his wife, Shoshana TelAviv. She started howling, hysterically.

"He's . . . he's dead!" replied Slavomir Propp, a large fat man with a bushy beard. He was a Russian professor of linguistics, who was a visiting professor at Berkeley that year . . . and who, the minute before, had been stroking Shoshana's right knee under the table. He was wearing a wrinkled blue gabardine suit that was two sizes too big for him.

"But this is absurd!" said Alain Fess, in a whiny nasal voice. He was a thin little man with a pointy nose and a scraggly beard. He was wearing a blue denim work shirt, a striped necktie, and blue jeans. "It is totally absurd." He was sitting between Propp and Myra Prail. "I think I'm going to throw up. . . ." Fess got up and ran off to a bathroom down the hallway.

"Well," said Basil Constant, the British novelist, in a calm and reasoned voice, "we'd better do something." He was sitting on the right of Myra Prail, between her and Miyako Fuji. Constant had gray curly hair and was wearing a fashionably cut double-breasted navy blue sport coat and gray slacks. Myra Prail,

Gnocchi's research assistant, said nothing. She had collapsed in grief, her head tilted back. Her long blond tresses hung down over the chair behind her. Her face had turned splotchy pink and her breasts, well displayed in the flimsy yellow voile dress she was wearing, were heaving.

And Miyako Fuji, seated to the immediate left of Gnocchi, stared blankly ahead, as if in a trance. Her glossy long black hair hung down to her waist. Her lips were covered with a pearly, translucent green lipstick and she was wearing green eye makeup. She was dressed in a tight-fitting green turtleneck and a short green skirt.

This macabre scene took place in the dining room at Gnocchi's and TelAviv's San Francisco home, a good-sized square room dominated by a large circular table. Two passages led from it—one to the kitchen and the other to the living room.

Basil Constant jumped up.

"We must get help!" he said. He ran into the kitchen and dialed 911.

"Hello . . . 911? Someone is dead! Someone is dead!" he shouted. "And it looks most certainly like he's been murdered. You'd best contact the police. I'm calling from the residence of Professor . . . that is, from the residence of the late Professor Ettore Gnocchi at 5000 Pacific Street in Pacific Heights. Yes, that's 5000 Pacific Street. Hurry!"

He placed the receiver down on the hook and returned to the scene of the death. Alain Fess had returned. He had a damp napkin with which he was dabbing water on Myra Prail, who was uttering low moans.

"Ettore . . . Ettore . . . dead. . . . No . . . it can't be."

"Please," said Fess. "We must not touch anything. We must just remain where we are until the police arrive . . . we must not disturb the evidence."

After the shock of Gnocchi's sudden death, Basil Constant noticed a slight trembling of his knees. Alain Fess suddenly felt sweat streaming from his armpits, wetting his blue denim shirt. Slavomir Propp could not restrain himself from a brief fit of wheezing and panting for breath. "Excuse me," he said. "I must use my inhaler." He rose and lumbered off to the bathroom.

Myra Prail had stopped crying. She had a look of sheer terror on her face. And Shoshana TelAviv moaned, as tears streamed down her face. Miyako Fuji stared ahead, blankly. She looked ready to faint at any moment.

The sound of a siren getting louder and louder could be heard . . . followed by the sound of a car screeching to a halt. Then came the sound of footsteps. After a few seconds there was a knock on the door. Fess got up and opened it.

A short, paunchy man, in a dark Harris tweed suit and a graying beard, strode into the room. He wore round tortoiseshell eyeglasses that were tinted a very light gray. His nose was fleshy; his eyes were bright blue and had a brilliant sparkle to them. They were eyes that were full of life, eyes that saw everything but revealed nothing. He was accompanied by a tall, slender man with a thin mustache. He had a sullen, rather pained look on his face. Behind them there were several policemen. The short man with the beard opened a leather wallet and showed everyone his badge.

"Police Inspector Solomon Hunter," he said. "And this is my assistant, Sergeant Talcott Weems."

"Take some photos, dust for fingerprints, and get the lab work done as soon as you can," Weems said to the policemen. "We'll want the results of the autopsy as soon as possible."

Hunter glanced at the body of Ettore Gnocchi, slumped over on the table . . . and then at the people sitting around the table.

"We did not disturb anything," said Alain Fess. "I learned we shouldn't touch anything from reading mystery stories."

"Will someone tell me what happened?" asked Hunter.

"It's like a nightmare," said Shoshana TelAviv. "All of the people here were helping my husband plan a scholarly conference. We were having a dinner party . . . my husband Ettore told me earlier that he had a surprise to announce . . . something very important."

"What was it?" asked Hunter.

"I don't know. Ettore wouldn't tell me. I had just brought out the dessert when the lights suddenly went out. It had been raining, off and on, and when this happens sometimes the electricity is interrupted for a minute or two. I heard a funny noise . . . like a hiss of a snake . . . just after I heard Ettore utter a soft groan . . . and then, when the lights went on after a minute or so . . . ."

She started sobbing.

"When the lights went on," said Propp, "Ettore was slumped over and he had a small bullet hole in the middle of his head. And there was a nasty-looking dart stuck in his cheek. And a knife in his back. . . ." He eyed the detective furtively.

Hunter looked at the body of Ettore Gnocchi. Then he studied the people sitting around the table. You had the feeling he was filing the image away in his memory. "Rather an odd little comedy I'm involved with here," he thought to himself. "One person who seems to have been killed four different ways at the same time." He was to remember that thought of his later.

"This scene is really quite amazing," he said. "In twenty-five years of investigating all kinds of homicides, I've never seen anything like this before." As he talked, the policemen who had come in with him were busy dusting for fingerprints and taking photos of Gnocchi and the room.

The people around the table were gazing intently at Hunter. He turned to Shoshana TelAviv.

"What was your husband's last name?"

"Gnocchi . . . Ettore Gnocchi was, quite likely, America's most famous postmodernist thinker. He had an international reputation. He was known all over the world. We were all helping him organize a conference on postmodernism that was going to be held at the Berkeley campus."

"I'll need to interview each of you separately," Hunter said. "If you could all wait in the living room, I'll find a place where I can talk with you."

He nodded to Weems. "Take them into the living room and get them settled while I find a place to interrogate them."

"You can use Ettore's study," said Shoshana TelAviv. "It's very private."

Sergeant Weems took everyone to the living room. After they had taken seats, Shoshana TelAviv led Solomon Hunter down a hallway to Ettore Gnocchi's study—a large room whose walls were lined from floor to ceiling with books. In front of a window there was a beautiful old oak desk. Next to it was a long table with a Macintosh computer, a Hewlett-Packard laser printer, a Xerox copy machine, and a Sharp fax machine on it. A few chairs were arranged around a marble coffee table and a sofa. A portrait of Gnocchi by Francis Bacon hung on one of the walls.

"He was really high-tech, wasn't he?" said Hunter. "Is that what postmodernism is about?" He paused, as if lost in thought. "Gnocchi. Somehow his name rings a bell, now that I think about it."

"I'm surprised you didn't recognize it," said Shoshana TelAviv. "He was really quite famous. Ettore was University Professor at Berkeley. He wrote more than twenty books. He used to be at Harvard, until Berkeley stole him away." With that she left.

Hunter looked around Gnocchi's study. It was full of books on postmodernism, literature, art, music, and philosophy. On Gnocchi's desk there was a pile of books by authors Hunter had never heard of . . . he glanced at some of them: Jean Baudrillard's *Simulations,* Michel Foucault's *The Order of Things,* Jean-François Lyotard's *The Postmodern Condition,* Fredric Jameson's *The Prison-House of Language,* Jürgen Habermas's *The New Conservatism.*

While Hunter was looking at the books, Weems came into the study.

"We found this note on Gnocchi's body," he said, handing Hunter a small envelope. Hunter read it aloud.

"I have reason to believe that my life is in danger. In the event I meet a violent death, it is the theory that will lead to my killer. It takes a theory to catch a theorist.—Ettore Gnocchi."

"Hmm," thought Hunter. "It seems that he knew that someone might try to kill him. Well . . . I think I'll take him up on his suggestion, and see what happens. I wonder why he didn't contact the police. Very curious."

"It *is* curious," said Weems. "But people generally don't take threats seriously. The same way they don't take the police seriously. They've read too many detective novels and believe that the police are all stupid blunderers."

Hunter said nothing, lost in thought.

Weems continued, "They're waiting for you to interview them. How are you going to go about it?"

"Let's start with Gnocchi's wife," Hunter said. "Dealing with scholars is very difficult. They're generally paranoid and highly manipulative . . . but, at the same time, intelligent enough to think things through, consider various contingencies, plan their moves carefully, and yet . . ." He paused for a moment. "Murderers always make mistakes. Something happens that they didn't plan on . . . there are crazy coincidences, accidents, that kind of thing.

"I'll interview everyone here," he continued, "and then we'll know more. And I'll see what I can learn about this post-modernism business. 'It takes a theory to catch a theorist.' That's what Gnocchi wrote, wasn't it? I'll find out, soon enough, whether he was right."

It [postmodernism] is also, at least in my use, a periodizing concept whose function is to correlate the emergence of new formal features in culture with the emergence of a new type of social life and a new economic order—what is euphemistically called modernization, post-industrial or consumer society, the society of media or the spectacle, or multinational capitalism.

Fredric Jameson, "Postmodernism and Consumer Society" (113).

chapter three

I'm an Israeli. I taught Political Science at Hebrew University for a number of years...

Shoshana TelAviv was the first person

to be interviewed. She had stopped crying but still had a grim, pained look on her face. She was a rather attractive woman, in her early fifties, with short light brown hair and luminescent blue eyes.

"Please tell me about yourself," said Police Inspector Hunter. "And about your relations with your husband. Were you getting along?"

"I'm an Israeli. I taught political science at Hebrew University for a number of years. Twenty years ago, I was teaching for a year in America at the University of Chicago and met Ettore at a philosophy convention. We were both interested in contemporary philosophical thought, and, in particular, postmodernism. Well, one thing led to another . . . we became engaged and a year later we got married. But I'm a modern woman, so I kept my maiden name, TelAviv."

"That was . . ."

"Nineteen seventy-six."

"Where did you live?"

"Ettore was, at that time, a professor of philosophy at Berkeley. He became University Professor a number of years later. I found Berkeley too provincial . . . the people there too serious about themselves, too caught up in their public passions . . . so we bought this house in San Francisco. All people talk about in Berkeley, it seems, is campus politics, real estate, and restaurants. I found it quite tedious."

"So you've lived here in San Francisco for the last twenty years?"

"Yes, except for occasional periods when Ettore was a visiting professor somewhere else."

"Did you continue to teach . . . or did you give that up?"

"I teach at Berkeley, also. But in the Political Science department. I've also been associated with the Cultural Research Center for many years. In truth, Ettore's interests and mine were quite similar. We were, as I said earlier, both interested in contemporary culture and postmodernism."

"I've heard that term before," said Hunter. "What exactly is postmodernism?"

Shoshana TelAviv smiled, weakly.

"It's not a simple matter. Ettore has written a dozen books on the subject, and I've written a couple on it as well. You might find it more instructive to look at them. In a word or two, postmodernism refers to the general contours of our culture for the last fifty years, give or take a decade. Or so a number of people argue."

She paused for a moment. "If you want to understand why American society is the way it is, you have to understand postmodernism and the influence it has had."

"Do you mean it's a philosophy? Or an economic system? Or an art style?" asked Hunter.

"Not at all. Postmodernism refers to what might be called a condition or theory, a collection of beliefs and values and attitudes that, though we might not realize it, shapes our consciousness and our society. We find it in the way we mix up different styles and genres in the arts and architecture. But it's not just an aesthetic . . .

it's a way of understanding the world and of living . . . though most of the people whose lives have been shaped . . . or perhaps *affected* is a better term . . . by postmodernism have never heard of the term."

She paused for a moment, as if to collect her thoughts.

"Maybe this will help," she said. "One of the leading postmodernist thinkers, the late French scholar Michel Foucault, was what might be called a perspectivist. Foucault pointed out that we don't live in a world of facts that have a meaning independent of people but, instead, in a world constantly subject to our ever-changing interpretations of it. There are many different interpretations of phenomena and, as the German philosopher Friedrich Nietzsche argued, there's no limit to the ways in which the world can be interpreted. So the more perspectives we have on anything, the more profound our knowledge and our understanding of it will be. Thus, postmodernism, in opposing unified and simplistic views of life and history, has in subtle ways shaped our contemporary consciousness."

"But how does it do this?" asked the inspector. "How does it shape our lives and our consciousness? All of this strikes me as pretty vague and nebulous."

"You're right," TelAviv responded. "Some theorists have suggested that there are so many different notions about what postmodernism is that the term is actually quite meaningless. People live their lives and do what they do based on what they see around them, based on what others do . . . most people don't think very deeply about matters like philosophy or metaphysics. But if a kind of belief system subtly underlies those actions, without calling much attention to itself, it doesn't mean that people aren't affected, even if they aren't aware of what is happening to themselves and to society.

"Postmodernism, you could say, is connected with the mass media revolution. The media are, to a considerable degree, postmodern now, and have a complicated relationship with society. The media both reflect certain aspects of society and at the same time profoundly affect society. This relationship ultimately leads to a radically different kind of consciousness—one that rejects the notion of progress, one that cherishes irony, one that revels in put-ons and superficiality, one that clips bits and pieces of things together, forming pastiches. Think of the way young children use remote-control devices to cruise the various television networks, creating their own programs out of bits and pieces of the programs they watch, making a postmodern media pastiche. In a modernist society, on the other hand, such as you Americans had in the 1950s or so, people would watch a program—such as a sitcom like I Love Lucy—from beginning to end. And we know that in those days, once viewers chose a program on a given channel, they often stuck with that channel for the entire evening. That just doesn't happen in the postmodern world of today, or with people who have a postmodern consciousness."

TelAviv paused to take a deep breath. "Well," she continued, "postmodernist thinkers will tell you that people living in postmodernist societies put their lives together in the same way, in bits and pieces, in fragments, just like artists do when they make pastiches. There's no coherence, no linearity any more. Reality is different for each of us, based on the experiences we've had and other matters such as where we were born and grew up, our gender, race, religion, and education. Nothing is simple anymore. There are no narratives that *mean* anything, and with the loss of narratives, our lives have lost meaning, as well. It's like a murder mystery that doesn't identify the killer for the readers." She paused again for a moment, then blanched, as if realizing what she'd just said.

"Speaking of murder," said Hunter coolly, "I'd like to ask some questions about your husband's death. Tell me, did your husband ever receive any threats from anyone? Has he received any recently?"

"Threats? Not that I know of."

"Was there any reason that you would know of that would lead him to suspect that his life was in danger?"

"His life in danger? He was a philosophy professor after all, not a talk-show host! Or a politician!"

"Did he have any enemies? People who really hated him?"

"Ettore?! That's ridiculous. Everyone loved Ettore. He was really a very sweet man. A very generous man, too . . . in every way." She spoke haltingly. Tears began to well up in her eyes.

"Of course," she continued, "as a philosopher and scholar, there were people who disagreed with him about a number of things. Some rather strongly. And he had an important position at the university. That always causes strained relationships . . . especially when it comes to personnel matters. But all of this is perfectly natural."

"Who are the other people here with you tonight?" the inspector asked.

"Ettore, as you might imagine, knows many people from all over the world," responded Shoshana TelAviv. "He had an international reputation and was often away, giving lectures at universities around the globe. He did make a point of asking me to have only these specific people here tonight to our dinner party, but they are all people we know very well."

"What can you tell me about them?"

"Alain Fess is a brilliant French sociologist, who wrote an important book on postmodernism and popular culture. Slavomir Propp is an internationally known linguist, who has done work on Russian tales and postmodernism. Basil Constant is a novelist whose work Ettore liked very much . . . Ettore saw Constant as another Italo Calvino, the Italian novelist. Myra Prail is . . . I mean . . . *was* Ettore's research assistant. She's working on her doctorate at Berkeley and writing on the relationship between capitalism and postmodernism. Ettore was her advisor. She's been his research assistant for several years, now. And the Japanese woman, Miyako Fuji, is a visiting professor this semester from the University of Tokyo. She's quite beautiful, isn't she . . . and, at times, very strange. She spends a lot of time staring at people. It's most disconcerting. When you get to know her, though, she can be quite voluble. She makes rather bizarre films, too."

"Let's return to the question I asked earlier," Hunter insisted. "How were you getting along with your husband?"

"What do you mean?"

"Nothing. I'm just looking for something to make sense of all this."

"We'd been married for twenty years . . . there have been problems, from time to time . . . you find that in any marriage. But I think you could say that we were happy. We still loved each other."

"You don't happen to know what your husband's big surprise was going to be? You don't have any idea, at all?"

"No, I'm sorry."

"How come none of your guests were here with anyone?" asked Hunter. "Isn't it a bit unusual to have a dinner party in which all the guests come by themselves?"

"Alain Fess isn't married. I believe he's divorced. But he's only here for a year . . . on some kind of grant. 'Soft money,' they call it. Slavomir Propp is divorced and has been for many years. He doesn't say much about his personal life. Basil Constant is gay, I think . . . or maybe bisexual? I'm not really sure about these things. Miyako Fuji isn't married, as far as I know. She's here at Berkeley by herself, so I assume she's single. She's very quiet . . . though, as I said earlier, when she starts talking, it comes out in torrents. Then she may become quiet again and say nothing for long periods of time. She's a very enigmatic person. And Myra

Prail . . . she's got loads of male friends, as you might well imagine . . . but she never brings any of them here when we have dinner parties."

"Do you have many dinner parties?"

"Yes. All of the people who are here tonight have been here almost every day for the past few weeks . . . working on an international conference on postmodernism that Ettore was organizing."

"Could you tell us what happened just before the lights went out?" asked Hunter.

"I had just served a chocolate mousse that I had made. We ran out of wine, so Myra went into the kitchen to get another bottle. Slavomir had brought a very large cake in a box. From Victoria Pastry, I believe. A giant panettone. He went and got it from the kitchen, just after Myra came in with the wine. That's about it. . . ." Her voice trailed off.

"Is there anything else you can tell us that might be useful?" asked Hunter.

"I . . . I can't think of anything. This has all been a bit . . . a bit overwhelming, as you can well imagine."

"What about Myra Prail? Am I to take it, from what you said earlier, that she sleeps around?"

"I said she has many friends. You might ask Basil Constant about her. I understand they've been spending a good deal of time together. She's using his novels in her dissertation, I believe."

"That's interesting," said Hunter. "One last thing—would you mind if I looked through your husband's files?"

"But isn't that somewhat indelicate? I mean . . ."

"Your husband was *murdered*, wasn't he? I want to find out who killed him. I assume you do, too. . . . You never can tell what you'll find when you look at a person's correspondence . . . and if you don't want to let me, I'll get a search warrant."

"Of course . . . I understand."

The postmodern as postmodernism is four things at the same time. First, it describes a sequence of historical movements from World War II to the present. . . . Secondly, the postmodern references the multinational forms of late capitalism which have introduced new cultural logics, and new forms of communication and representation into the world economic and cultural systems. Thirdly, it describes a movement in the visual arts, architecture, cinema, popular music, and social theory which goes against the grain of classic realist and modernist formations. Fourthly, it references a form of theorizing and writing about the social which is post-positivist, interpretive, and critical. Postmodern theorizing is preoccupied with the visual society, its representations, cultural logics, and the new types of personal troubles (AIDS, homelessness, drug addiction, family and public violence) and public problems that define the current age. . . . But postmodernism is more than a series of economic formations. The postmodern society, as suggested above, is a cinematic, dramaturgical production. Film and television have transformed American, and perhaps all other, societies touched by the camera, into video, visual cultures. Representations of the real have become stand-ins for actual, lived experience.

Norman K. Denzin, *Images of Postmodern Society: Social Theory and Contemporary Cinema* (ix–x).

chapter **four**

Alain Fess couldn't sit still for a second.

He played with his necktie; he fidgeted; he drummed his fingers; he crossed, then uncrossed, his legs. And he talked rapidly, hardly stopping for a second . . . as he eyed Solomon Hunter with furtive, sideways glances.

"I can't tell you how *horrible* this has been," Fess said, tugging at his scrawny beard. He didn't have a mustache; just a thin, scrappy beard that made its way, hesitantly, down his face from his cheekbones to his chin. "Ettore was, of course, a dear personal friend. I had grown really fond of him, and Shoshana as well, during my stay here. But more than being a personal loss, Ettore's death is a terrible loss to society . . . and to the university . . . and to the world of ideas. He was a giant . . . as you would know, if you had read any of his books."

"When did you meet him?" asked Hunter.

"Many years ago. Our most recent meeting was when he gave a lecture on postmodernism a few years ago at the CNRS . . . that's a French national research institute. A number of us went out for dinner afterwards. Baudrillard, Bourdieu, and Levinas were there . . . and we had a marvelous discussion. And, of course, a really superb meal. You know, of course, how good French food can be. That's why we like to come to Berkeley . . . the food. And the coeds. I've always loved Berkeley."

"I don't know any of those names," said Hunter.

"Why should you?" replied Fess. "They're all scholars, philosophers, and sociologists from France . . . only if you were an academic, or an intellectual, might you know of these people. Or if you read the *New York Review of Books,*" he said with a crooked smile. He had a way of talking without looking directly at the person he was talking with.

"I am a sociologue . . . I mean, *sociologist,*" said Fess. "But my particular interest is in contemporary trends in society, and so, quite naturally, I became interested in postmodernism. You must remember that we French, from de Tocqueville on, have a history of explaining America to Americans. We love to do it, too. We like the rawness, the energy, the exuberance, the lack of taste and sophistication in America. And we also like the big steaks.

"There's a lot of talk about the sense of superiority that French people feel about 'French civilization and culture,' " he added. "But superiority to Americans? No, not at all. It isn't that we French feel superior to Americans; we feel superior to everyone."

He paused for a moment to laugh. It had a forced quality to it. He fumbled around in his pockets and eventually found a handkerchief with which he started wiping his face. Then he started scratching his right knee.

"What we find in America, which is why it fascinates us so much, is the *future.* America represents the future and, alas, we fear France will eventually, perhaps soon, become like America. That is why we are so interested in your shopping malls, your hamburger restaurants, your crazy hotels, your pop artists, your films, and your television shows. It is your media, your society of

simulations and pseudo-simulations and virtual realities and make-
believe that fascinates us so much.

"America is the most well-developed postmodern society,"
Fess went on, gazing into the middle distance, "and all of us who
are interested in what the future holds are drawn irresistibly, as a
moth is to a flame, to America. And what's most interesting is that
Americans don't know what they've done, don't realize that, in
their invincible ignorance, they have created the quintessential
postmodern society. That is why French sociologists and philosophers are so important. We have a history of explaining America to
Americans. I and my colleagues, in a sense, are descendants of de
Tocqueville. For the twentieth century, though."

"Tell us about this conference on postmodernism that
Gnocchi was planning," said Hunter. "His wife mentioned it."

"It was my book, which was translated into English as
Minotaur: The Beast in the Shopping Mall, that led Gnocchi to ask
me to help him with the conference. My book is my analysis of the
Mall of America in Minnesota. Ah, such a place! . . . the largest
mall in America . . . with an amusement park in the middle of it.
Amazing! But I stray. Ettore planned a conference in Berkeley with
many of the leaders of postmodern theory from all over the world.
He had some kind of a grant from the university to help him with
some of the expenses. We were involved in arranging a date, decid-
ing who would speak, developing the theme of the conference . . .
that kind of thing."

"Who had you contacted?" asked Hunter.

"We were, as you would say, rounding up the usual sus-
pects," said Fess, laughing. "Through my intervention, on his
behalf, Ettore was in contact with the French postmodernist
Mafia—Baudrillard, Lyotard, Deleuze, Lacan, Kristeva, and
Derrida. Also Eco in Italy; Jameson, Rorty, Spivak, Poster, and
Kellner in America; Habermas in Germany. The names you see all

the time in the bibliographies at the end of books on postmodernism. There's a small group of us who make the circuit; we write for each other's journals and we give lectures at each other's conferences."

"What can you tell me about Gnocchi?" asked Hunter.

"What do you mean?" replied Fess.

"For starters, how was he getting along with his wife? How was he getting along with the others at the dinner party?"

"You ask difficult questions," Fess answered, taking out his handkerchief again and mopping his brow. "More difficult than you can imagine. I can speak as someone who has spent a good deal of time with Ettore and Shoshana and all the others in recent months. But I can only surmise certain things . . . I can only make inferences . . . do little more than make some guesses; but guesses, of course, often have an element of certainty about them, about their very insubstantiality, do they not? The guess as the guess is sometimes correct but at all times firmly seated in the realm of the hypothetical."

"Hmm," thought Hunter. "These French intellectuals live in a world of their own. Most of the time it's impossible to tell what they're talking about. Maybe all the time?" He paused for a moment. Fess wasn't firmly seated. He was fidgeting around, scratching his nose, and swinging his right knee, which was crossed over his left leg.

"OK. Make some guesses," said Hunter, thinking this was going to be a long night.

"I'm reasonably confident of this: Ettore's wife, Shoshana, has been having an affair with that blimp, Propp. I can't imagine what she could see in this man—though, of course, his work is, I must admit, first-rate."

"How so?"

"Propp's book, *Morphology of Modernism,* is probably the definitive work on modernism—that's the period roughly from the mid–nineteenth century, starting with Baudelaire, to the Second World War. In modernism, there's a rejection of traditional narrative structure, the linear sequence of events we find in stories of various kinds—fairy tales, myths, and novels—in which there is a beginning, middle, and end. That's what Aristotle wrote about. This linear structure is replaced by a fascination with paradox, illogicality, uncertainty, and montage. Things are, how you say? . . . stitched together to generate emotional responses, but there is not the traditional concern with sequence and logic. People in modernist works are not seen as whole but as fragmented and dehumanized. You see this in the works of the great modernist writers and painters—in Joyce, Musil, Mann, Yeats, and Faulkner, in Picasso and Matisse and Braque, in the Dadaists and Surrealists. Consider, for example, the surrealists. They rejected logical and linear narratives and emphasized, instead, the world of the imagination, the world of dreams, the world of the unconscious. It was stream of consciousness, not consciousness, that interested the surrealists. As well as modernists of all kinds."

"So postmodernism is a rejection of modernism?"

"Precisely. Postmodernism means, if you take it literally, 'coming after' modernism, and figuratively, rejecting modernism. Postmodernism rejects the so-called difference between elite art and popular culture; it emphasizes eclecticism in art styles, ironic stances toward life, superficiality instead of depth, the role of reproduction as against originality in art . . . that kind of thing. What you find in Laurie Anderson, Warhol, Pynchon, Cage, Stockhausen. Postmodernists blur the distinction between reality and fiction or nonreality; they mix genres, revel in irony and 'put-ons' and the mass-produced."

"But isn't all this about art and literature, more than anything else?" asked Hunter.

"No, not at all," replied Alain Fess, sweating a bit less and easing into his role as pontificator and explicator. "The subject is, of course, very complicated . . . and many postmodernist thinkers disagree with one another about what postmodernism is and which artists and writers qualify as 'postmodern.' But all of these artists and writers and musicians are like a rash from poison ivy, reflecting something going on in the body below the surface."

"Speaking of poison," said Hunter, "do you have any notions about who might have wanted to kill Gnocchi? Who would gain from his death? That kind of thing."

"Shoshana and Propp may have been having an affair . . . but people—at least people in France—don't kill one another over affairs, as a rule. You know about affairs . . . they start, the heat is great, the passion formidable . . . and then comes the coolness, the boredom. And then the next affair. Marriages are modernist; affairs are *post*modern."

"So you don't think his wife or Propp is involved?"

"I don't know. Propp is an important writer and thinker. I can't imagine he would do something so absurd over a woman. But who knows? He's a perfect beast as a human being, once you dig beneath that facade of amiability, and is probably capable of anything."

"What about Myra Prail?" asked Hunter, consulting his notes.

"Myra is a gorgeous woman, but she's not too bright. Very calculating, though. Very determined. She seems to have a way of getting what she wants."

"And this, uh, Miyako Fuji?" he asked, mangling the pronunciation.

"She seems very strange when you first see her," Fess replied, "the way she sometimes stares at people. When you get to know her, as I have, however, she's quite lively and she has a fantastic imagination. I think she's really a lovely person. Of course, she tells incredible tales about everyone. How she gets her information is beyond me. She probably makes it all up. She may be a pathological liar? She's taken lately to making obscure films."

"I'm looking for a motive for this murder," said Hunter.

"But you do not understand," said Fess, looking at Hunter with the look professors have when they are asked to explain something simple, for the fifth time, to a dull student and have the feeling that nothing they say will make the slightest difference. He raised his left hand and, poking his index finger in the air, said, "You are a prisoner of your modernist categories and psychology. In postmodernist murders, motives are absolutely *irrelevant!*"

Between word and image, between what is depicted by language and what is uttered by plastic form, the unity begins to dissolve; a single and identical meaning is not immediately common to them. And if it is true that the image still has the function of speaking, of transmitting something consubstantial with language, we must recognize that it already no longer says the *same thing*; and that by its own plastic values painting engages in an experiment that will take it farther and father from language, whatever the superficial identity of the theme.

**Michel Foucault,
*Madness and
Civilization: A
History of
Insanity in
the Age of
Reason* (18).**

chapter **five**

"How can I help you?" asked Slavomir Propp.

He was holding a brown cigarette, pointed towards the ceiling, between his thumb and first two fingers, the way many Eastern Europeans do. He wore tinted blue glasses in thin gold frames. He was flabbily fat, with bulbous pink cheeks and lips and chins and a great, soft egg of a belly. His face had a porcine quality about it: he had dark, beady, pig-like eyes and a giant snout of a nose.

"Is that your full name—Slavomir Propp?" asked Hunter.

"Actually," Propp said, after taking a puff from his cigarette, "my first name is Vyachislov. But I've never liked the name, so I use my middle name. Besides, Americans find Vyachislov too difficult to pronounce. The French, too. Most people do—except for Russians and Poles."

"Alain Fess has spoken very highly of your work," said Hunter.

"He did?" said Propp, with a surprised look on his face. "I was always under the impression that he didn't think much of it. Or maybe it was that he didn't think much of me."

"Why do you say that?"

"Alain is, first and foremost, a Frenchman. And you know the French. . . . France is really a third-rate power, but the French act as if France were the center of the world. For Parisians, every-place more than five miles from the center of Paris is 'the prov-inces.' And the French are like the Parisians in that respect—there is France, and then there is everyplace else. That pose of superi-ority, that endless refrain about French culture . . . it gets quite tedious, if you know what I mean.

"And the bread in France is no longer very good. That's important," Propp rambled on. "So Alain has this French attitude . . . but also, he's a rather pompous little man, too. He wrote one fairly decent book and has leveraged it into an endless number of grants and conference appearances. He is an anxiety-ridden, nervous little man who is, I believe, capable of anything."

Propp took another puff from his cigarette and blew some beautifully formed smoke rings up toward the ceiling.

"The French have a few good philosophers nowadays," he went on. "Most of them are Jews, by the way. It's the Jews who are the thinkers in France, for the most part. French culture nowadays is the culture of the Eastern European yeshivas, one generation and a thousand or so miles removed. The best French thinkers are all the sons or grandsons of rabbis. Aside from the Jews and some good restaurants, and leftovers from earlier periods, like the chateaux and some castles, the French are *nothing*. Have you ever looked at the monstrosities the contemporary French architects have created? France, like most European countries, is living off the past. France is good for naive tourists, but little else. Western Europeans, you must realize, for the most part are not serious thinkers . . . and are not serious people. They have become obsessed with amusing themselves . . . rather like the Americans. To tell you the truth, the French bore me to death!"

"Speaking of death," said Hunter laconically, "tell me what happened tonight, in as detailed a way as you can."

"It's a mystery to me," said Propp, shrugging his shoulders. He looked at Hunter through his blue glasses, his beady little eyes trying to size him up. There was intelligence in those eyes . . . but was there something else? Something menacing beneath the pose of the jolly fat man? Hunter wondered.

"The other day," Propp went on, "Ettore invited me to dinner here at his place. We ate dinner together often, you know . . . we were planning a conference . . . but I believe you know that. In any case, we were having dessert when suddenly the lights went out. It had started storming a few minutes before and was very windy. It's not unusual for the lights to go out for a moment or two . . . or sometimes for a whole day when the weather is stormy. Trees fall over and disrupt the power lines. The electric company in Northern California is notoriously bad about keeping its lines operating. Being from San Francisco, you know that, surely.

"But when the lights went back on," Propp continued, "a minute or so later, Ettore was slumped over, the way you saw him, with that bullet hole in his head and that horrible dart sticking out of his cheek. It was quite shocking. Basil Constant called 911 and a short while later you and your colleagues arrived. We don't know much more than you do."

"What about the cake you brought?"

"Oh, yes . . . I had brought a large panettone—you know, that delicious tall cake-bread with raisins and pine nuts—from Victoria Pastry. Ettore was Italian, as you know, and loved panettone. I had left the panettone in a box in the kitchen. So I went to fetch it. Myra Prail had gone into the kitchen to get another bottle of wine and our paths crossed. I had no sooner brought the panettone back and sat down to slice it, when the lights went out."

"What were you going to use to slice it?"

"Good Lord!" exclaimed Propp. "A silver knife . . . a stiletto. I used it all the time, when I brought cake. The knife was in the center of the table when I last saw it, if I remember correctly."

"How come you used that knife?" the detective asked.

"Shoshana had bought that knife for Ettore for his sixtieth birthday. She said it had sentimental value for her. She is, you should know, very emotional and very affectionate."

"Tell me," said Hunter, "how did you fit in with this little group of postmodernists? I'm getting all kinds of different ideas about what it is. Everyone seems to have a different perspective."

"But of course," said Propp. "You realize, no doubt, that academics tend to disagree with one another on just about everything . . . and that the academic world is full of little cliques of fellow travelers and believers who spend all their time attacking those who have different beliefs—sometimes in a rather bland and gentle way, and at other times in personal and even vicious and violent ways. Professors may be intelligent, but they aren't always nice. But after all . . . we are human, and humans are not always gentle creatures. Remember what Freud said . . . 'Man is a wolf unto other men.' "

"Some professors aren't even smart," Hunter said. "I can remember some I had who didn't have any common sense and struck me as rather stupid."

"Agreed, agreed. But that is the human condition. Not everyone is intelligent; think how terrible the world probably would be if they were."

Propp blew some smoke rings in the air.

"My particular aspect of postmodernism, to answer your question, has to do with narratives."

"Narratives?"

"Narratives. But narratives, let me remind you, are not just simple little stories that we read in books or see in films and television programs. We learn a great deal about life, as well as death, from narratives; and here in America, where most people watch television for at least four hours a day, they are exposed to an incredible number of narratives. People in other countries may not watch as much television as Americans . . . yet. But they are catching up. Our lives tend to merge with the television programs we watch—with commercials, soap operas, situation comedies, action adventure stories . . . the list is endless. And these narratives, these simulations, tend to have a subversive effect on people. We become very much like ghosts, like spirits, with no lives and no emotions of our own. We have emotionless lives because we experience all our emotions second-hand, through the characters we watch on television and in films. Why have your *own* emotions when an actor or actress can do it for you?

"What I have worked on," Propp added, "is what makes a narrative a narrative, and also on the impact that narratives have upon us, as individuals and as members of society. I am a theorist of narratives; and this is important because in postmodern societies, as some have argued, people no longer accept meta-narratives— philosophies and things like that, which tell everyone what they *should* be doing—and have, instead, turned to their own lives, or what might be described as their private and personal narratives."

"I've got a pretty good idea of what you mean by narratives," said Hunter, growing more interested in the discussion, "but what are meta-narratives? I'm not sure what the term means. I've never heard it before."

"Many postmodernist theorists argue that in postmodern societies we have abandoned the great overarching philosophical belief systems that used to explain things for us—such as Marxism, which explained how society took the form that it did, or Freudianism, which explained how the human psyche worked, or myths, which explained how humans were created. These belief systems, which we call meta-narratives, either are no longer accepted or are questioned. But the problem is that without them, how do we make sense of both ourselves and society?"

Propp paused to let the question sink in, and blew another puff of smoke into the air, which was now getting quite blue. "When we lose narratives," he went on, "we lose our sense of ourselves, and we also lose what narratives give us—a sense of the *meaning* of life, an understanding of the world and our place in it. Without narratives, life is merely a random succession of events leading nowhere. There's no beginning, no ending . . . just experiences."

"But if people reject these meta-narratives," asked Hunter, "reject the philosophies and religious beliefs and political ideologies that enable people to live with one another without spending all their time fighting or killing each other, how do you avoid anarchy?"

"Precisely. What has happened is that postmodernism has destroyed our heroes, and now it's dissolving our narratives as well. And what is to take the place of these heroes and their narratives? Since the forties and fifties, when postmodernism started to show itself in modern societies, *all* our institutions have been in crisis. In America, more than anyplace else, people distrust authority of all kinds, and there is a crisis of legitimation. That is, we no longer feel that our institutions, such as government and education, are legitimate or that we have obligations to them. This contagion is spreading. Alexis de Tocqueville coined the term *individualism,* which, in terms of my interest in narratives, suggests that only individual, personal, private narratives are important. But what do you get when the public narratives, which have socialized and encultured people, are thrown on the ash heap of history? Well, you get lives or private narratives that, as Hobbes put it, are 'nasty, brutish, and short.' "

"So postmodern societies reject abstract theories, over-arching belief systems, and—" Hunter began, and was interrupted.

"As Lyotard put it, postmodernism can be defined as 'incredulity toward meta-narratives.' Another central tenet, which comes from Nietzsche, is that there are many different ways of seeing things . . . that everyone sees things in terms of his or her own interests, taste, background, education, social situation, and so on. We all become, in a sense, prisoners of ourselves and our private passions."

"That's quite a mouthful." Hunter was beginning to wonder if he'd ever find out who murdered Ettore Gnocchi.

"Yes, but it does capture the essence of the argument," Propp went on. "We are incredulous, at best, about the meta-narratives or philosophical systems that formerly structured our lives, in earlier decades. Thus, postmodernism is reflected in the eclecticism we find in our lives today. We patch together a per-sonal style, on the basis of momentary whims, different fashions, cuisines, hair styles, kinds of music, sexual partners . . . all of this is possible, of course, only as long as one has money. Money is the only absolute, the only standard that is left in postmodern socie-ties. In all other areas, anything and everything goes."

"Where does love fit into all of this?" asked Hunter.

"Love? What's love got to do with it? Love is a modernist abstraction. Postmodernists are more concerned with sex . . . and, of course, violence. And I, I must confess, am not a stranger to violence. Before I became a scholar I was, for a number of years, a spy—working for Section K of OGPU in the Kremlin. In that capacity I was required to do some . . . shall we say . . . rather nasty things. I have stolen some interesting information . . . and have had material stolen from me, as well. But I have, of course, put all that behind me."

Propp gave a half-hearted laugh.

Hunter looked at Propp, who had taken another cigarette from a package and was lighting it. "Propp is an enigmatic figure," he thought. "He's a huge, flabby person and yet, those eyes . . . and now, it turns out, he's been a spy, a member of OGPU. Why would he volunteer that information? Maybe because he figured we'd discover it ourselves? This way he's inoculated himself. Is he terribly shrewd or just being open and matter-of-fact with me? Is he playing games with me? Spies are difficult to deal with. They're all paranoid. With good reason, of course. It comes with the job."

He thought for a moment, then asked, "Are you having an affair with Gnocchi's wife?" Hunter looked intently at Propp to see how he would react.

Propp's face gave nothing away. He laughed. "Me? With Shoshana? Where did you possibly get that crazy idea?!"

"In my business we get lots of ideas . . . they're in the air."

"I flirt with her, I must admit. . . . She's still a very attractive woman and a very loving woman, too. And a terribly smart woman, as well. But the idea of my having an affair with Shoshana? That's preposterous."

"What about Myra Prail?"

"What would a beautiful young woman like that see in an old fat Russian? I'm probably forty years older than she is. Besides, I've heard she has a very active social life and has lots of men who are pestering her, all the time. You can understand why. She's not only beautiful, but extremely intelligent . . . and very determined, as well. Yes, a very determined young woman."

"What about that Japanese woman, Fuji?" the detective asked.

"Miyako? Miyako is an exotic porcelain doll. She's all intellect. She's hollow . . . she's got this beautiful exterior, but there's nothing inside. She has absolutely no emotions—at least, as far as I can tell. Of course, we've only been working together with Ettore for a few months. She may be crazy . . . she says strange things and makes incredible films."

"What about Ettore himself? Could he have been fooling around with Myra or Miyako? You know what they say about power being the ultimate aphrodisiac."

"But Ettore was a serious scholar . . . and he was married to a lovely and charming woman. Why would he possibly do anything like that? Especially at his age." Propp fell silent.

"I thought you postmodernists liked eclecticism and variety," Hunter said. "And more old men than you might imagine like to fool around with young women . . . and do so when they get the chance!"

"Ah," said Propp, suddenly becoming animated. "I see what you have in mind. And if a young and beautiful woman has, perhaps, some kind of a psychological complex and is searching for . . . shall we say a lost father. . . ."

"A powerful older man who can open doors—to good jobs as well as bedrooms—becomes rather appealing. Maybe for only a short period of time, but that time can be thought of, if you're really cynical, as having been well invested," said Hunter. "And, of course, some young women actually like having sex with older men."

"Yes, yes . . . I see what you mean," said Propp, becoming even more animated. "I see what you mean." He took a drag on his cigarette and blew some beautifully formed smoke rings in the air. He stabbed a plump index finger through one of the smoke rings.

"I'm sure you do," replied Hunter.

Herbert W. Simons and Michael Billig, *After Postmodernism: Reconstructing Ideology Critique* (6).

The problem is not that the postmodernist spirit lacks a critical impulse, but that critique is running rampant without political direction. Zygmunt Bauman, in *Intimations of Postmodernity,* describes how the new mood can appear to be one of "all-eroding, all-dissolving *destructiveness*" (1992:viii; emphasis in original). He goes on: "The postmodern mind seems to condemn everything, propose nothing," as if "demolition is the only the job the postmodern mind seems to be good at" (p. ix). The genie of critique has escaped its bottle, and now, unstoppably, it darts hither and thither in random flights of mischief. It does not merely attack the ruling ideas, or the mass-produced ideas of economically organized popular culture. What Paul Ricoeur (1986) calls the "hermeneutics of suspicion" has become the prevailing mood. Every assertion of truth is to be the target of critique, for every such assertion, so it is alleged, makes claims which cannot be substantiated. Moreover, it is an exercise of power, for each claim about "the true," or "the real," asserts its own voice, and thereby suppresses alternative voices.

chapter six

Myra Prail looked terrible.

Her eyes were bloodshot, her hair hung in tangles over her shoulders, her skin was pale and still blotched pink. She had put on a red Stanford University sweatshirt. She walked, unsteadily, into the room and sat down on a chair.

"God," she said. "How horrible! Poor Ettore."

She glanced at Solomon Hunter, as if she were trying to figure him out, discern his vulnerabilities, find a way to somehow deal with him. It was the same look professors get from their students when they walk into the classroom for the first time. The students may have heard something about the professor, may have talked with other students who have studied with him or her. But each professor is an enigma, a mystery, a puzzle to be solved, a person to be probed for weaknesses and vulnerabilities by each student.

"I can see that Professor Gnocchi's death really was a shock to you," said Inspector Hunter, scrutinizing her. "You seem to be taking it harder than the others. Why is that? And how come the others seem to be so sanguine? So much in control of themselves? Do you have any notions?"

49

"I really . . . I really don't know," said Myra. "I truly loved Ettore . . . he was such a sweet man. He was so funny, so full of life."

"How long had you been his assistant?" the detective inquired.

"For three years. I'm just finishing up my dissertation this year. I've started looking for a job . . . and Ettore was helping me. He has . . . I mean he *had* a lot of contacts, as you might well imagine. He knew everyone."

"What are you doing your dissertation on?"

"Its title is 'Capitalism and Postmodernism: A Marxist Perspective.' I'm taking Fredric Jameson's notion that postmodernism is really the name for culture in the latest stage of capitalism and is connected with the rise of the multinational corporation and the relationship between these corporations and our military-industrial complex."

"Who's Jameson?" the detective inquired, wondering if the man could be another suspect in the murder.

"A Marxist who teaches comparative literature at Duke. He's written *The Prison-House of Language* and a classic book on postmodernism, *Postmodernism or the Cultural Logic of Late Capitalism*, and many other books. He argues that postmodernism is not just aesthetic and stylistic promiscuity but, in reality, a stage in the development of capitalism that manifests itself in the cultural realm. Of course, the theory is very controversial. I'm arguing, like Jameson, that narratives still exist . . . but they have gone, so to speak, underground and now are lodged in what you might call everyone's political unconscious. Of course, the Freudians on campus here are having absolute fits! Fortunately, I don't have any of them on my thesis committee."

"Let me get this straight," Hunter said, stopping her. "This Jameson believes that postmodernism doesn't represent a break in history, a break with modernism? That's just the opposite of the notion I got from talking with Shoshana TelAviv, Alain Fess, and Slavomir Propp. I was led to believe that postmodernism is something new, something radically different. And now you're telling me it isn't, that it's just one more stage in the development of capitalism?"

"Yes, that's right," Myra Prail responded. "Of course, some philosophers and theorists argue that postmodernism is now dead, and has been for a long time . . . and that we are in a stage that can best be described as *post*-postmodern. Others, especially in Germany and the Scandinavian countries, argue that we never really were in a postmodern stage but that contemporary cultures are actually all late modernist ones . . . and have been for the past fifty years."

"I don't see the sense in all this," Hunter said, beginning to get a bit perturbed. "Why do so many people spend so much time and energy arguing over things that strike me, and would probably strike most people, as trivial? Where does this late modernism versus post-postmodernism debate get us?"

"Tell me, Inspector," Prail said calmly. "Do all police agree on everything? Don't some police want to build more prisons, and don't others think we have to *do* something to prevent at-risk young people from becoming criminals? And don't some detectives do things differently from others?"

"Yes, of course."

"Well, it's the same with the postmodernism debate. We're all trying to get at the truth, to the extent one can say there is such a thing as truth, and trying to make sense of things as best we can. If you think of postmodernism as being like a disease, we're like doctors who are trying to figure out what the disease is, what caused it, and what we can do to cure it. The problem is, there can be many different causes for a particular disease, or, in some cases, one disease can have many different symptoms. Or think of society as being a murder mystery . . . and, like you, we're all detectives trying to solve it."

Her chat with Hunter had calmed Myra Prail. The color had returned to her face and she seemed much more relaxed, much more at ease. She leaned back and crossed her extremely shapely legs.

"What can you tell me about Gnocchi's wife, Shoshana TelAviv?" The inspector launched a new line of inquiry. "Did Gnocchi and she get along?"

"Yes, they got along quite well. They were married a long time. But there were complications, you must understand."

"What do you mean?"

"I probably shouldn't say this . . . but I assume you'll find out sooner or later." She paused and leaned forward. "Ettore confided in me one day, when he was really upset about Shoshana."

"And what was it he told you?" asked Hunter.

"Shoshana was unfaithful to Ettore . . . many times."

"How did he take it?" asked Hunter.

"He was devastated. What hurt him most was that Shoshana was having an affair with Alain Fess!"

"Fess?"

"Yes. You must realize that Fess had been a student of Ettore's a number of years ago."

"I didn't know that."

"Yes, he got his degree under him. And Ettore played a big part in bringing him to Berkeley for this year . . . to work on the conference. And then, the next thing you know, Alain and Shoshana are . . . are . . ."

"Screwing each other."

"Well, yes, though that's a somewhat indelicate way of putting it."

"I had the funny idea that Shoshana and Propp were having an affair."

"Propp? Shoshana and Propp? He's brilliant but he's really rather gross . . . and very mixed up, psychologically. He's quite paranoid."

"How so?"

"Propp's most famous book is *Morphology of Modernism*—and it's a very fine book, I must admit. Slavomir told me that he was convinced that Ettore stole his ideas and used them in his masterpiece, *The Postmodern Prisoner*. 'I had let Ettore read a manuscript I was working on,' Propp said, 'and a year later, before I could publish my ideas, *The Postmodern Prisoner* appeared.' Of course," said Myra, "I didn't believe him. I can't imagine that Ettore would do anything like that. It doesn't make sense. But Slavomir was very angry. Think about it . . . if Ettore had stolen Slavomir's ideas, why would Slavomir agree to work with him? And why would Ettore *want* him to? I concluded, then, that Slavomir had a tendency to imagine things and that his story about his ideas having been stolen by Ettore was far-fetched."

"So you don't think that Propp and Shoshana are having an affair?"

"I don't know . . . but it strikes me as quite preposterous. It's Alain Fess that she's involved with, I believe. Ettore's former student. At least that's what *Ettore* thought."

"What do you know about Miyako Fuji?"

"Very little. Somebody—I don't remember who—told me she was a lesbian. But I have no way of knowing, of course. She's a strange woman, though. I imagine you could sense that right away. The Japanese, you realize, have a tendency to push things to extremes. I've always felt that Japan is even *more* of a postmodern society than America."

"Could you explain?"

"Just look at Tokyo. It's an absolute horror—a mixture of gigantic skyscrapers and little back alleys where people are still living in the nineteenth century. The people in Tokyo have no room to live, so they live in hyperreality. They spend half their time shoving little balls down pachinko machines. . . ."

"What about you? I've got the notion that you aren't the kind of girl you pretend to be. Are you having an affair with any of the people who were at the dinner table?" The detective watched her face intently.

"Me?!" Myra Prail exclaimed, laughing. "But they're all, except for Alain, two or three times as old as I am. Why should I be interested in any of them? I have lots of attractive men my own age to keep me company. Alain is boring and Slavomir is an ugly, fat old man. And Basil is gay. I spend a lot of time with him because I'm writing about his novels. And he's nonthreatening, if you know what I mean."

"That leaves Ettore. What about him?"

Myra Prail turned bright red. "Ettore? Me and Ettore? You think Ettore would get involved with one of his students? Take advantage of his power? Not Ettore. He was from the old world and had a highly defined moral sensibility. Even though his wife was cheating on him, Ettore did not cheat on her."

"How do you know that?"

"I don't. Not for certain. But if you knew Ettore, you'd understand why I don't think Ettore was cheating on Shoshana, though it would have been perfectly understandable if he had."

"You think one good deed deserves another?"

"No, I didn't mean it that way. I'm getting all confused," she said. "I meant that given the fact that Shoshana was cheating on Ettore, it would be understandable for him to cheat on her. It wouldn't have been the right thing . . . but you know human nature."

"But I thought postmodernists didn't *believe* in human nature," Hunter said. "I've been led to believe here that the idea that there's something called human nature is a metaphysical idea . . . or, should I say, something that people who are incredulous about meta-narratives couldn't possibly believe."

"For a policeman," Myra Prail said, "you've got some pretty interesting ideas . . . and a pretty good notion of what postmodernism is."

"Why shouldn't I?" replied Hunter. "Look at the wonderful teachers I have."

As with the pairing of modernity-postmodernity, we are again faced with a range of meanings. Common to them all is the centrality of culture. In the most restricted sense, modernism points to the styles we associate with the artistic movements which originated around the turn of the century and which have dominated the various arts until recently. Figures frequently cited are: Joyce, Yeats, Gide, Proust, Rilke, Kafka, Mann, Musil, Lawrence and Faulkner in literature; Rilke, Pound, Eliot, Lorca, Valery in poetry; Strindberg and Pirandello in drama; Matisse, Picasso, Braque, Cézanne and the Futurist, Expressionist, Dada and Surrealist movements in painting; Stravinsky, Schoenberg and Berg in music. . . . There is a good deal of debate about how far back into the nineteenth century modernism should be taken (some would want to go back to the bohemian avant-garde of the 1830s). The basic features of modernism can be summarized as: an aesthetic self-consciousness and reflexiveness; a rejection of narrative structure in favour of simultaneity and montage; an exploration of the paradoxical, ambiguous and uncertain open-ended nature of reality; and a rejection of the notion of an integrated personality in favour of an emphasis upon the de-structured, de-humanized subject. . . . The problem with the term [postmodernism] . . . revolves around the question of when does a term define oppositionally to, and feeding off, an established term start to signify something substantially different?

Mike Featherstone, *Consumer Culture and Postmodernism* **(7).**

chapter seven

What's this obsession you have about who Fess is sleeping with??

If Basil Constant was gay,

he certainly wasn't easy to spot as such. He was tall, slender, and very well dressed . . . in a casual way. And he wore his clothes beautifully: a double-breasted navy blue blazer and dark gray slacks.

"Are you a professor?" asked Inspector Solomon Hunter.

"Heavens, no!" said Constant. "I have no desire to spend my life teaching students who are bored or stupid—and sometimes both. I have taught an occasional creative writing class here and there, but I found it, as a rule, terribly tedious."

"Why did you teach creative writing, then?"

"The money. You chat with some students a bit about creativity and read a bit of a short story or a few pages from some novel-in-progress that your students pass in at the end of the semester, and you get paid rather handsomely for your efforts. The money comes in handy between novels."

"Where have you taught?"

"When I lived in Boston I taught a course at Harvard. And I've taught an occasional course for the New School in New York. I didn't mind that. And I spent a *horrendous* year at the University of Iowa at the workshop they have for writers there. I will admit there were a few interesting people around the university . . . but can you imagine what it's like living in a small university town like Iowa City and being entirely surrounded by cornfields?! The nearest big city is Des Moines, where there are only three or four decent restaurants. That's what Iowa is like. It's corn before culture in Iowa, even though the people in Iowa City delude themselves and call Iowa City the 'Athens of the Midwest.' What nonsense. New York is a thousand miles away.

"Chicago is fairly accessible, but I never liked Chicago. In Iowa City I always felt I was in some kind of prison . . . one in which there are no walls, or windows with bars.

"Speaking of bars," Basil said, interrupting himself, "there were, fortunately, a few decent bars there. But Iowa was impossibly cold in the winter and there was no spring. When I was living there, one day the snow melted and the next day the sun came out and it became unbearably hot and humid. Like living in a blast-furnace. Fortunately, I escaped from Iowa with my sanity . . . or so I think.

"I also taught for a few semesters at California University in Los Angeles, but I found the place terribly depressing. For the most part, the students were either ignorant or apathetic—and in some cases, again, they were *both*. The president and provost and most of the deans spent all their time, it seems, looking for other positions, but never were able to find them. The faculty hated the administration and acted like prisoners, serving out their time.

"It had once been a rather exciting institution," the professor continued, "or so I understand—but from what I saw of it, it has fallen on bad times. One faculty member told me that I should really think of California University as a country club—it has a nice swimming pool, it has tennis courts, and so on. You teach your classes and then spend the rest of your time at the pool, playing tennis or whatever.

"I found it more like a prison or a morgue. The teaching load wasn't bad, but the place had a depressing ambience . . . spoiled kids and frustrated faculty members. Most of the students seemed to be interested in having fun in their fraternities and sororities and going to the beach in Santa Monica or wherever. The student culture was incredibly anti-intellectual, with just a small, saving remnant of interested students. Of course, that's the way it tends to be in many schools."

"How long have you been living in California?" Hunter seized the chance to interject a question.

"More than a dozen years. After Iowa and a short time in Los Angeles, I came here and decided to stay put in San Francisco. It's really the only decent city in America. It has a good symphony, an excellent ballet, a first-class opera company . . . and many excellent restaurants and bars. Most of the cities in America are either insanely difficult to live in, like New York, or so dull that you could die of boredom."

"Speaking of dying," the detective murmured, laconically, "who do you think killed Ettore Gnocchi?"

"Inspector . . . I don't *know* who killed him—and I don't know *why* whoever it was who killed him killed him. That's what you're supposed to find out, isn't it?"

"Yes."

"And how are you progressing?"

Hunter smiled wearily. "It's hard to say, right now. But tell me . . . what's your connection with Ettore Gnocchi and his little band of postmodernist professors? You're a novelist. Why were you here tonight?"

"I've written more than a dozen novels. Two of them are considered postmodern classics. Or, perhaps, to be a bit more modest, minor classics. One is called *Chameleon* and deals with the way people change their personalities to blend in with wherever they find themselves, thus becoming difficult to see, if not invisible. My hero had no identity, in the sense that identity is something that involves continuity. He was like Woody Allen's Zelig. When Zelig was with Chinese people, he looked Chinese. When he was with Germans, he looked German. The title of my other novel is *Constrictor*. Its hero fights against the institutions of the modern state, which, if you catch my metaphor, coil themselves around us and smother us. Resistance is possible, I suggest. This is a Foucaultian position, I might add. The boa constrictor is, of course, modern science and the various scientific disciplines and other kinds of knowledge that seek to regulate us, keep us under surveillance, monitor us and control us. There are ways, however, of subverting the modern state and its institutions, of keeping the constrictor in its cage where it belongs. My books were published in England, where they got excellent reviews, even if they didn't sell particularly well. The *Times Literary Supplement* described *Constrictor*, if you'll pardon my quoting from memory— and I have a stupendous memory for blurbs—as 'a masterpiece of contemporary fiction that offers hope for resistance against the dominating institutions of society and a chilling picture of the alienation that exists in contemporary society . . . alienation that the hero of this tale helps overcome.' " Basil paused to take a big breath. "My book definitely had a Foucaultian slant."

"Who's Foucault?" Hunter seemed to recall that Gnocchi's widow had described, rather fulsomely, someone by that name.

"Foucault? He was one of the greatest thinkers in postwar France, the author of books such as *The Order of Things*, *Madness and Civilization*, *The Birth of the Clinic*, and *The Use of Pleasure*. He was a real giant—one who was influenced by Friedrich Nietzsche and thus wrote from what could be described as a perspectivist view."

Basil Constant was warming to his topic. "In essence, what Foucault argued was that there are no facts, only varying interpretations of the world. Nothing has a single meaning; things must be understood in terms of the many different ways that exist of looking at them. And the more perspectives you have on anything, the better it is, because that means you can have a deeper understanding of it. My description of Foucault's perspective is pretty abstract, of course . . . but I would hope you get the general idea."

Hunter wasn't sure that he had. But he asked, "So you have the same notions as Foucault? And your novels established you as a 'postmodern' writer?"

"Yes. Some people thought my *Chameleon* had the same kind of sensibility in it that James Purdy's *Malcolm* has. Are you familiar with him? He's a very important contemporary American novelist."

"No, I've never read anything by him. I don't get the chance to read much fiction in my line of work."

"Maybe your life is so exciting, Inspector, that you don't *need* to read fiction?"

"Maybe." The detective wondered, with a little stab of annoyance, if Basil was putting him on.

"Well, I'll tell you, in brief, about this classic. Malcolm, the hero of Purdy's novel, is a young boy who's living in a fancy hotel in Florida. He is sitting on a bench outside the hotel, waiting for his father to come back and fetch him. The father, of course, never appears. Malcolm meets someone who introduces him to a really extraordinary collection of characters—before he gets married to a rock singer and, while still very young, screws himself to death. Pardon my French," Constant added with a wry smile.

"Do you think Gnocchi could have screwed himself to death?" Hunter was seeing a theme. "Or could it be that his screwing around led to his death?"

"I catch the drift of your comment . . . but I really can't say. You might want to read *Malcolm*. The story is simple . . . but it's Purdy's style, his use of grotesques, and the surrealistic, nightmarish ambience of the story, with its decentered hero, a hero without a coherent identity, that gives it a postmodern cast. Or you might like Thomas Pynchon's *The Crying of Lot 49*, a really remarkable existential picture of Southern California life that suggests that there's a secret, unofficial post office system working in America, used by certain secret groups of people. The notion that there's a hidden reality that we don't perceive, this mysterious post office system, attacks our sense that we know what's going on as well as our belief in the legitimacy of our institutions. That's quite postmodern," Constant said with a flourish.

"And Pynchon, get this, has never been seen by *anyone*," he continued. "He refuses to be photographed. He's invisible—like the hero of my book, who's a chameleon and who is very difficult to see. It's a study in camouflage, really, which is not the same thing as invisibility. And, of course, there's the great postmodernist novel *Invisible Man*, about a black man who is 'invisible' to whites.

You know, there are actually some people who think that I'm Pynchon. The idea, of course, is ridiculous. I'm British and I know very little about what Americans are really like."

"You wouldn't learn too much about America from Ettore and the group of people he assembled around him to plan the conference, would you?"

"What do you mean by that?"

"Well, except for Myra Prail, none of them are Americans, I believe. Isn't that curious?" Hunter realized he had yet another clue to pursue. "Ettore Gnocchi was Italian, Shoshana TelAviv's an Israeli, Alain Fess is French, Slavomir Propp is Russian, Miyako Fuji is Japanese, and you're English—well, British, as you say."

"That's true, but you have to realize that the really great educational institutions are, by nature, international. Like the great football—or what you would call *soccer*—teams. World-class scholars move around from this university in Paris to that university in England to another university in America all the time. Berkeley is the greatest public university in America, and probably in the world. So at any one time, its faculty has many visiting professors and permanent professors from all over the world. And a large number of the graduate students at Berkeley are from abroad, as well. We mingle together and love one another, and in some cases, marry one another . . . it's only natural."

"Are you married?" asked Hunter.

"Me?" Constant laughed. "I was married, years ago, for a rather short while. But it didn't last. I was too young to know myself . . . or know any better. I'm afraid I'm really not what you'd call the marrying kind . . . though marriage has its attractions, I will admit."

"Like what?"

He laughed. "Mainly, someone to eat out with. It's so tedious eating by yourself in restaurants, if you know what I mean. Also to help you as you keep on reinventing yourself. If you're by yourself, you don't know whether your latest reinvention really works. You need someone else to help you *know* yourself." Constant wondered how the detective was taking all this self-portraiture.

"Tell me about Gnocchi's wife, Shoshana. How well do you know her?"

"Shoshana's a lovely woman. Warm, nurturing, and actually quite brilliant. I always thought Shoshana was much smarter than Ettore. She has an extremely logical, analytical mind . . . the kind that can plan and execute anything, that sees the pitfalls in philosophical arguments, that can anticipate intellectual problems before they arise. And yet, when you talk with her, she comes across as quite an *ordinary* woman. You'd never realize how accomplished she is, nor how sophisticated."

"Someone told me that she's been having an affair with Fess. How does that strike you?"

Constant laughed. "Fess and Shoshana? Ridiculous."

"Why do you say that?"

"Shoshana might be motherly to Alain, perhaps . . . and affectionate to him. But Shoshana sleeping with that twit Fess?! The idea strikes me as simply preposterous."

"What about Fess and Myra Prail?"

"What's this obsession you have about whom Alain Fess is sleeping with?"

"I'm just looking around for information," Hunter responded, to calm his subject. "That's what I feed on. I'm trying to find out who's done what to whom. There were six people and

Gnocchi at the table when he was killed. Someone at that table killed Gnocchi, and I'm trying to find out who it was. I'm looking for motivesand they come from relationships between people—from fights they have, from jealousies, from anger about slights that fester for years or decades, from men who jilt women and women who jilt men. You're a novelist, Mr. Constant. You should, I imagine, know about such things. You should know about motives and the dark side of the human psyche. Isn't that what you write about?"

"Yes, of course. That's what *most* writers deal with. But it strikes me, Inspector, that you're grasping at straws, that your imagination is running away with itself."

"You think so? Let me give you some crazy ideas," said Hunter. "And tell me what you think of them. Number one: Fess is sleeping with Shoshana and they decided, irrational as it might seem, to get rid of her husband. There could be a million reasons why. Number two: Ettore Gnocchi was having an affair with Myra Prail. You could understand why he might want to. She's a really beautiful young woman . . . and he's a powerful figure who can help her in any number of different ways. Number three: Shoshana and Propp are having an affair. It would seem ridiculous, but these things happen. Maybe Gnocchi found out about it and threatened to cause trouble? Number four: Alain Fess and Myra Prail are having an affair. She can see living in Paris with a rising star in French intellectual life. Doesn't seem so bad. Maybe Gnocchi found out about them? That wouldn't be a problem, would it, unless Gnocchi was in love with Myra? You know what they say—there's no fool like an old fool. Wouldn't a Gnocchi–Prail scenario be interesting?"

"Almost as interesting as the four ways Ettore was killed," said Constant, with an irritating glee.

"Yes," said Hunter. "That's an important point, of course. Maybe Shoshana and Propp decided to kill Gnocchi. They wouldn't know, would they, that Alain Fess and Myra Prail had also decided to kill him. Or maybe the four of them got together to kill him. There has to be more than *one* murderer, I'd say."

"And then," Hunter went on, "there's also the possibility that Shoshana TelAviv, or Fess or Propp, or Myra Prail is having an affair with more than one person?"

"Why not?" said Constant. "The idea of a person having affairs with two or three people strikes me as being in the best traditions of British democracy."

"Then there's *you*," said Hunter, looking at Constant, who at that moment pulled himself up in his chair. "God only *knows* which of these people you might be involved with. Or maybe you're involved with more than one of them at the same time? It's been known to happen."

Basil Constant laughed. If he was nervous, he didn't show it. He looked Solomon Hunter directly in the eye.

"You really have a remarkably vivid imagination, Inspector. I don't know whether to describe it as feverish or wild. If you weren't a police officer, I might suspect you were on drugs. You see affairs everywhere, you find conspiracies among everyone. Have you ever thought of writing novels? You have the mind for it and I think you'd be good at it." Constant paused to reflect. "Yes . . . you might have the makings of a first-class novelist. You have characters doing all kinds of improbable things, you mix them up in bizarre relationships . . . all you need is to make your characters into grotesques, add a touch of surrealism to destroy the traditional novel's narrative coherence, and you could be an outstanding postmodern novelist. You've got the feverish imagination."

"It's not a matter of imagination," said Inspector Solomon Hunter. "Haven't you heard? Truth is stranger than fiction. Even postmodern fiction!"

Loss of the real induces a "panic" reaction, in which nostalgia blooms, cults of authenticity arise and the (post-)culture abandons itself to the "panic-stricken production of the real. . . ." Baudrillard argues that the secret of Disneyland is that it has to be presented as "imaginary" to preserve the fiction that America is "real". . . . Kroker and Crook . . . apply these themes in television so that "Television is, in a very literal sense, the real world . . . of postmodern culture, society and economy." Just as the effaced hyper-reality of Disneyland is necessary to preserve the "reality principle" of America, so a variety of ideologies and practices efface the circumstance that "it's not TV as a mirror of society but just the reverse: *it's society as the mirror of television."* Television enacts the postmodern "precession of simulacra" in which "it is the map that engenders the territory." (Baudrillard 1988: 166)

Stephen Crook, Jan Pakulski, and Malcolm Waters, *Post- modernization: Change in Advanced Society* (68).

chapter **eight**

The "porcelain doll," Miyako Fuji,

sat down stiffly and stared at Solomon Hunter. She was obviously nervous.

"Hmm," he thought. "She's either extremely shy or extremely troubled." He wondered which it might be.

"What can you tell me about the events that have just taken place?" asked Hunter.

"You'll excuse me," she said in a voice that was just above a whisper. "I've not been sleeping well lately. My work has not been going well. . . . And now, this horrible thing that happened to Ettore. . . ."

"I understand," said Hunter. "Relax. I'm just trying to get whatever information I can. You never know when you'll pick up some thread that will lead you, eventually, to the killer."

Fuji shuddered when she heard the word. "That word . . . it's so cold . . . it scares me. But America is a violent country. In America people are always getting killed—and if people are getting killed, that means other people are their killers."

"You're a visiting professor here, from Tokyo University. Is that right?"

"Yes." She sat, looking at him, with her body strangely twisted, as if she were trying to get as far away from Hunter as possible.

"Is this your first visit to America?"

"No, not at all," she said. "I've been here many times."

"Why?"

"I received my Ph.D. in America. American doctorates are highly esteemed in Japan. Especially from first-class universities."

"So that's why you speak English so well. Now I understand. Where did you get it?"

"Oh, I'm sorry. I thought you knew. I got it here at Berkeley. Ettore Gnocchi was my dissertation adviser."

"What? Gnocchi again?" He seemed slightly shocked by her last statement. Then, after a few seconds, he said, "I see. I'm beginning to get the picture."

"I was a year behind Alain Fess. He took his doctorate here, too. And Ettore Gnocchi was his dissertation adviser, as well."

"So you've known Alain Fess for a long time."

"Yes, I most certainly have," she said, smiling weakly. "You see, Alain and I were once married."

"Married? You and Fess?"

"But only for a few years. We broke up . . . but we're still good friends. It was that . . . well, probably the best way to explain is to say that we found out that we just weren't suited for one another."

"You . . . married to Alain Fess? I never would have imagined such a thing."

"Why not?"

"I can't put my finger on it," the detective replied. "There's something about Fess that's a bit off, if you know what I mean. He's got a crooked smile. He never looks at you eye-to-eye when he talks with you."

"Actually, Alain is a very sweet man, who's suffered a great deal."

"Suffered?"

"Yes. Ettore almost drove Alain to suicide. He didn't tell you about it?"

"No. But I was under the impression, from Shoshana TelAviv, that Ettore was a kindly and gentle person whom everyone loved."

"Ettore—kindly and gentle?!" She laughed. "Ettore was a monster. He chewed up graduate students, stole their ideas, and then spat them out. He abused all his men students and seduced . . . I mean, *tried* to seduce all of his women students. Ettore only *seemed* kindly. It was a mask, his persona. The kind Italian papa who drank Chianti with his students. He often had his students over for dinner. But not to eat with them—it was to *devour* them. Under the kindly mask, the real Ettore, in his privatissima, was a monster. He was a snake."

"But what about Shoshana? Didn't she know what was going on? Didn't she object?" Hunter asked.

"Why should she? She happens to like young men—and Ettore, one way or another, provided any number of them for her."

"What? Are you telling me that he procured students to sleep with his wife?"

"Yes. Her sexual appetite is, how should I put it . . . enormous. She's insatiable . . . she's almost as bad as Myra Prail, who's got very round heels. Myra's actually been diagnosed as a nymphomaniac. She's very beautiful, which helps her enormously."

"Someone told me that Alain Fess and Shoshana were lovers. Is that true?"

"For a long time."

"And Gnocchi didn't care?"

"Gnocchi and Shoshana had what people describe in America as an open marriage . . . in the best postmodern tradition. She paid no attention to his predatory behavior with his women graduate students and young faculty members—since he provided her with so many attractive young men. You have to realize, when Shoshana was younger she was quite beautiful . . . and she can be very enticing. It was a most remarkable marriage, even by post-modern standards."

"And what about you and Gnocchi? It's an indelicate question, but it's an important one."

"I . . . I must leave that to your imagination," she said, halt-ingly. "Let me say that Ettore has a very powerful and a very seduc-tive personality . . . and that I was. . . ." Her voice lowered to a whisper . . . "I was . . . to my shame, I was. . . ."

She stopped speaking and started trembling. Tears were welling in her eyes.

The detective paused to consider, then asked: "If Gnocchi was a monster, how come so many people worked with him? How come so many of you who have been his victims have returned to Berkeley to help him put on his conference?"

"Because Ettore was also extremely helpful. He arranged for us obtain fellowships and grants, he found us appointments at good institutions, he helped us publish articles and books. All he asked, in return, were some sexual favors. And remember, in postmodern societies like America, where traditional morality is one of the meta-narratives that has been discarded, sex is now just a commodity. It is a sign of your alienation."

"What do you mean?" Inspector Hunter was beginning to sense a tangled web indeed.

"Love has been incredibly devalued . . . like the money here. In all too many cases, one has sex with the same degree of passion and involvement that one exhibits in ordering a Big Mac or a Whopper. And morality now is just a hollow word. Everyone's a predator, and when they're not predators, they're victims. It all works out beautifully. We end up with, it turns out, the *worst* of both worlds—predatory victims, and victimized predators.

"It's the same way in Japan," Miyako continued. "Even worse, because Japan is a claustrophobic, hermetic society. The old population clings to myths from our medieval past, while the young population is increasingly punk and postmodern. And alienated. That goes without saying. That's why we have so many 'love hotels.' They really are temples for alienated sex. Samurai dreams and postmodern, alienated sex. . . ." Her voice trailed off.

"You're painting a rather depressing picture of America and Japan," said Hunter.

"That may be because I'm depressed myself, Inspector. Depression may be a postmodern condition. Or it may be a disease to which numerous intellectuals . . . or perhaps postmodern intellectuals in particular . . . are vulnerable. Sometimes I suspect that doing a great deal of thinking isn't *good* for us—that we're not meant to privilege thinking. That may be why Zen is so popular. The medieval Zen teachers, you may not realize, were clowns, and they posed problems that showed the limitations of thinking. When they asked, 'What is the sound of one hand clapping?' they really were asking us to question the power of rationality."

"But if you don't believe in rationality, what do you believe in?"

"That's a question my students in Tokyo often ask. It has puzzled philosophers for ages. I believe in nothing. Life is meaningless." Miyako Fuji bit her lip, and fell silent.

Hunter thought for a moment, and then pursued his line of questioning: "All of you who are here tonight, except for Constant, who's a writer, and Fess, who's a sociologist, are philosophers. Is that right?"

"Yes. Propp is a linguist, but the line between linguistics and philosophy often disappears."

"And all of you are, to one degree or another, involved with this postmodernism business. But, as I understand it, there's a lot of disagreement about what postmodernism is and what its impact has been." Hunter looked at Miyako Fuji with a puzzled look on his face. She had stopped staring at him, for some reason.

"That's correct," she answered, "but that's true about *many* things in universities. We battle over ideas and theories and we write articles and books to show that those who don't believe the same things that we do are wrong, and those who believe what we believe are right. But most people are like that, if you think about it. In universities we use our minds and we use words to battle with one another. In the so-called real world, beyond the walls of our universities, individuals fight with one another, countries declare war on one another."

"And people kill one another, too," interjected Hunter.

"Yes, of course," said Fuji. "In the final analysis, naturally, it isn't mind, but *power* that is the determining factor in most relationships."

"You're interested in power?" Hunter could hardly believe where his questions were taking him.

"Very much. You see, I'm trying to synthesize postmodern thought and feminism. And all feminists are interested in power, but they don't want to use it in masculinist, phallocentric ways."

"I'm not sure what you're talking about," Hunter said, turning a little pink around the collar.

"Let me start at the beginning, Inspector. We make sense of the world by using language and concepts. Now Saussure, one of the most important linguists of the twentieth century, explained that concepts only have meaning differentially, in being, as he put it more or less, what their opposites are *not*. So we make sense of things by setting up, in our minds, at every instant and very rapidly, polar oppositions—happy and sad, rich and poor, nature and culture . . . the list is endless. We do not do this consciously, I should add. Concepts have meaning, then, because of their relations with other concepts . . . the most important relationship being, of course, opposition. What feminist postmodernists argue is that the most central opposition found in society is based not on class but on gender."

"Gender is more important than class? So feminists aren't Marxists?"

"Some are—but a person's socioeconomic class identity can change, can't it? A person is born into a poor family, invents something or strikes oil, and ends up very wealthy. But one's sexual identity is immutable . . . we are all locked into our genders by nature. Except, of course, for a number of transsexuals, male and female. So what we feminists argue is that sexual conflict, conflict between men and women, is more basic than conflict between members of different socioeconomic classes. And the most important hidden theme in history, we suggest, is that of the domination and subjugation of women by men."

"But how does feminism relate to postmodernism. . . . I don't see that."

"Both are, in the final analysis, criticisms of society. Postmodernists argue that the traditional narratives, what some of us call meta-narratives, that have legitimized our institutions and social arrangements are no longer believed in, and feminists argue that these narratives are, implicitly and often explicitly, sexist. Because women become, generally speaking, mothers, their identity and their sense of self is by nature, one might argue, relational. Women, you could say, are designed to gain their identities through relationships with others, such as their babies and children and other women, and they are also temperamentally constrained to want communities where their children will be nurtured and they will be protected. Men, on the other hand, develop their sense of self by separation and estrangement from others and, in many cases, from society."

"So, for feminist postmodernists, the differences between men and women are really enormous," said Inspector Hunter.

"Yes, in terms of both sexual identities and the political power that stems from these differences. Freud asked what women wanted. He thought they wanted penises . . . but the answer is simple—woman want equality and justice and a sense of community to help us develop ourselves and raise our children. But it's very hard to obtain these things in a world dominated by men."

"Am I correct in assuming," asked Hunter, "that your feminist ideas are connected in some way with your relationship with Ettore Gnocchi . . . and maybe even Alain Fess?"

"Of course," replied Miyako. "Personal experiences lie behind and shape most philosophies . . . though, of course, as a postmodernist, I find it hard philosophically to justify generalizations. That's the dilemma we face. How do you justify any belief without recourse to logic, to other beliefs, to narratives and meta-narratives? Our incredulity toward the meta-narratives of others doesn't extend to our own meta-narratives."

"So feminists want to have their cake and eat it?" Hunter blurted out.

"Just like predators," she replied, enigmatically, "of either sex."

As opposed to the seriousness of "high modernism," postmodernism exhibited a new insouciance, a new playfulness, and a new eclecticism embodied above all in Andy Warhol's "pop art" but also manifested in celebrations of Las Vegas architecture, found objects, happenings, Nam June Paik's video-installations, underground film, and the novels of Thomas Pynchon. In opposition to the well-wrought, formally sophisticated, and aesthetically demanding modernist art, postmodernist art was fragmentary and eclectic, mixing forms from "high culture" and "popular culture," subverting aesthetic boundaries and expanding the domain of art to encompass the images of advertising, the kaleidoscopic mosaics of television, the experiences of the post-holocaust nuclear age, and an always proliferating consumer capitalism. The moral seriousness of high modernism was replaced by irony, pastiche, cynicism, commercialism, and in some cases downright nihilism.

Douglas Kellner, "Postmodernism as Social Theory: Some Challenges and Problems" (239).

chapter nine

The problem is that nobody seems to agree with anyone about anything!!

After Miyako Fuji left,

Solomon Hunter sat thinking for a while. He had a puzzled look on his face. He was trying to digest what he had heard, and figure out what kind of a person Ettore Gnocchi really was—and, above all, whose story, among each of the suspects, he might believe. Or which parts of them.

"The problem," he thought, "is that nobody seems to agree with anyone else about anything. . . . Each of the people around the table, all of them postmodernists, told different stories." He couldn't help but chuckle. "But isn't that one of the things postmodernism teaches us . . . incredulity toward meta-narratives and, in fact, all narratives? Maybe the perspectivist position of these postmodernists isn't so far-fetched? Maybe the solution is to get as much information as I can and then see what it tells me? Maybe Nietzsche's ideas had some merit and will help me solve this case?" He felt as if he had just been forcibly enrolled in graduate school, and had to study furiously to catch up.

He decided to look around Gnocchi's study. The books in his library were mostly on philosophy—in German, Italian, English, French, Spanish. Gnocchi had written a lot of books and they were randomly placed, here and there, on different shelves. There also were reprints of some books that Gnocchi had written, translated into half a dozen languages, including Hebrew, German, Italian, Japanese, Chinese, and Korean.

On a couple of large shelves, Gnocchi had copies of forty or fifty dissertations by his students, and in some cases, books that came from the dissertations, generally with an introduction by Gnocchi. Hunter looked at who had written the dissertations.

Turning to his right, he noticed a large metal filing cabinet with five drawers. In it were files on all kinds of abstruse subjects: metaphysics, architecture, semiotics, linguistics, archaeology. . . . Hunter pawed through folder after folder, looking for clues that would help him understand this man. Gnocchi had files with his book contracts, files with his royalty statements, files on places he'd traveled, files on courses he'd taught. It was in the middle drawer that Hunter found something that looked interesting—a thick file marked "Printouts of Conference Letters/Copies of (1995/1996)" containing printed letters from Gnocchi's computer.

"I think I'll take a look at what Gnocchi was writing to his friends," thought Hunter, as he pulled the file out of the filing cabinet. "I've heard a lot about Gnocchi from others. Now, let me see what he has to say for himself."

Eclecticism is the degree zero of contemporary general culture: one listens to reggae, watches a western, eats McDonald's food for lunch and local cuisine for dinner, wears Paris perfume in Tokyo and "retro" clothes in Hong Kong; knowledge is a matter for TV games. It is easy to find a public for eclectic works. By becoming kitsch, art panders to the confusions which reign in the "taste" of patrons. Artists, gallery owners, critics and the public wallow together in the "anything goes," and the epoch is one of slackening. But this realism of the "anything goes" is in fact that of money; in the absence of aesthetic criteria, it remains possible and useful to assess the works of art according to the profit they yield. Such realism accommodates all tendencies, just as capital accommodates all "needs," providing that the tendencies and needs have purchasing power. As for taste, there is no need to be delicate when one speculates or entertains oneself.

Jean-François Lyotard, *The Postmodern Condition: A Report on Knowledge* (76).

chapter ten

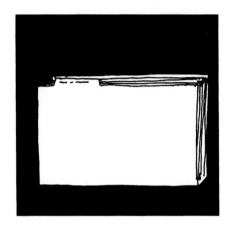

Hunter pulled out a number of letters

from the file. The first one he looked at was to Jean-François Lyotard.

```
March 11, 1996
Dear Jean-François:

     I'm glad you'll be able to attend the
forthcoming conference in Berkeley. It will be
good to see you again. And how is life in Paris?
     Your book The Postmodern Condition: A Report
on Knowledge is still considered one of the clas-
sics, even though you wrote it in 1984. I hope the
Canadian government, which commissioned the work,
appreciated the enormous significance of your
report. It has been required reading for those
interested in postmodernism for many years.
     We haven't decided what to call the confer-
ence. How does "Postmortem for Postmodernism"
strike you? This will enable us to consider
whether postmodernism is still a vital force or
whether it has, as some have argued, become passé.
The people who are funding this conference—a
number of different foundations—will feel very
good, I'm certain, that you will be speaking.
```

You, of course, will be the star attraction,
being, in my opinion and the opinion of many
others, the most important contemporary theorist
of postmodernism. Jean Baudrillard will be there
also. He's become quite impossible lately—maybe
all that adulation from the Americans has gone to
his head? He's been to too many conferences in
America, I'm afraid, and received too much uncriti-
cal adulation. We will humor him, of course, and
avoid getting into arguments about his notions
on reality and hyperreality. Leave that for the
Americans. The other main speakers will be Jürgen
Habermas and Fredric Jameson.

In your talk I'd like you to deal with
your notion that the term *modern* refers to any
realm of knowledge that tries to gain acceptance
by allying itself to a grand narrative or over-
arching philosophical theory and that postmodernism involves a rejection of meta-narratives,
which are now obsolete. Then I hope you'll deal
with the problem of legitimation, the way meta-
narratives have tended to legitimate or justify
the state and traditional social, as well as
political, arrangements. And, of course, I'd
like you to speak about the role narratives play
in the scheme of things.

You've been attacked by critics who argue
your notion of postmodernism leads, ultimately, to
social atomization and anarchy, perhaps even to a
breakdown in our social institutions and our legal
order. But I don't believe that's your position at
all. This erroneous characterization of your ideas
is connected, as you rightly point out, to fantasies or to myths (that may be a better term) that
people have about ancient, so-called "organic" or
naturally integrated communities.

In postmodern societies, if I understand
your argument correctly, it is the narratives
that people share and their bonding as these
narratives are recited, written in stories
and novels, or acted out in plays, films, and

television stories that hold them together. I think, for example, of all the movies that have been made out of characters from the comics and of the interesting phenomenon of movies now being made from situation comedies from the sixties and seventies, which enable our children to relive, in a sense, our childhoods—or more precisely, the narratives of our childhoods.

It is not abstract and abstruse totalizing principles and theories—which are, as you put it, really "concealed narratives," not valid at all times and in all places—that create societies. It is the narratives that we listened to, read, or watched and that we share with one another that are crucial. I'd like you to deal with this matter in your inimitable style.

That is why, as you suggest, popular narratives and popular culture in general are so important. Of course, the grand narratives or metanarratives still have lost their credibility, even when they are the theme of popular narratives, because, as you rightly make clear, these narratives contained within them the seeds of their own destruction and delegitimation. Legitimation really comes from people having common language practices, common language games, and common narratives, and our ability to pull things together from many different areas of knowledge.

Finally, I'd like you to deal with the impact of postmodernism on society, with the changes it is bringing about in our institutions, in culture, in our sexual practices, in the family, and in politics. It is in this area that people often get confused. They may understand, on a high level of abstraction, what postmodernism is; but the problems arise when it comes to seeing how postmodernism has shaped our social institutions and our culture, shaped the way people see things and then act, and of course shaped the work of our artists and writers and playwrights.

You've written about the eclecticism that
we find in contemporary cultures—we eat McDonald's hamburgers for lunch, we listen to reggae,
we watch westerns, dab ourselves with French
perfumes in Tokyo, and wear retro clothes in
Hong Kong. I'm counting on you at the conference
to make the connections between your theories
and our everyday lives.

Baudrillard and Habermas and the others
I've invited are, as you well know, utterly
unpredictable. But *you,* I know, I can count on.

Alain Fess is here for a year. I helped him
get a grant to come to Berkeley, but he's pretty
useless. I think I made a mistake in bringing him
here. He's been riding his book, really quite a
minor work, for all it's worth...but I think people are now tired of him. He whines too much. I'm
afraid he'll have to resign himself to being only
a secondary source, not an original and primary
thinker.

You remember Slavomir Propp, no doubt. He's
here, too. He's gained a great deal of weight in
the past few years. He keeps himself together
with a huge belt around his stomach. If that
belt breaks and his flesh is let loose, I think
his stomach will cascade down to his ankles and
he'll simply unravel. At least he has a sense of
humor. The problem with linguists is that they
think that every discipline is a subspecialty of
linguistics. Linguists are all snobs. They take
after their master, Jakobson. But Roman was a
man of tremendous accomplishments; his work on
metaphor and metonymy and his elegant model of
the communication process have established him
as a true giant. Harvard did well when it lured
him there. Most of the contemporary linguists
are only mediocrities. Snide and self-satisfied
mediocrities, but mediocrities nevertheless.

There's an interesting writer who's been
hanging around, Basil Constant. He likes to

think of himself as the English Calvino, though he's not in the same league as Italo was, by any means. Still, Constant has written some decent novels and you might enjoy meeting him. He's got that Oxbridge presence about him. You know—he's very smooth, has excellent manners, and has a nice gloss on him. You wonder what's inside, though. That's something of a mystery.

We also have Miyako Fuji here, from the University of Tokyo. If I recall correctly, you've reviewed several of her books in the *Times Literary Supplement*. Have you met her? I'm not sure. She's a bit strange...has a tendency to stare at people. I wonder, at times, whether it's some kind of psychological problem or whether she's having mild seizures...she's also quite lovely and delicate, the way Asian women often are. She dresses stylishly and very dramatically—if you know what I mean. She speaks in a whisper most of the time. Once you get to know her, though, she comes out of her cage and is quite sociable. I think she may be a lesbian, but I can't say why I have that notion. She's taken to making films lately. They're quite bizarre.

Finally, I have a wonderful research assistant, Myra Prail—the best one I've had in *years*. Every fantasy that people have about American women is realized in Myra. She's got long blond hair, blue eyes, a gorgeous figure. She's a beauty queen who's doing her thesis on postmodernism. She's absolutely brilliant...and ruthless, as well. You'll love her, I'm sure of that. And she's very friendly, too. But you must be very careful with her. Take my word for it.

You'll stay with us, of course. Shoshana sends her love.

— Ettore

Post-modernity is neither optimistic nor pessimistic. It is a game with the vestiges of what has been destroyed. This is why we are "post"—history has stopped, one is in a kind of post-history which is without meaning. One would not be able to find any meaning in it. So, we must move in it, as though it were a kind of circular gravity. We can no longer be said to progress. So it is a "moving" situation. But it is not at all unfortunate. I have the impression with post-modernism that there is an attempt to rediscover a certain pleasure in the irony of things, in the game of things. Right now one can tumble into total hope-lessness—all the definitions, everything, it's all been done. What can one do? What can one become? And post-modernity is the attempt—perhaps it's desper-ate, I don't know—to reach a point where one can live with what is left. It is more a survival amongst the remnants than anything else.

Jean Baudrillard,

"On Nihilism"

(38–39).

chapter **eleven**

The second letter Ettore sent was to Jean Baudrillard

at his address in Paris.

March 11, 1996
Dear Jean:

When I told Shoshana that you were coming to my conference, she was absolutely delighted. You know how fond Shoshana is of you. During our last trip to Paris it was delightful getting together with you. We enjoyed that strange little Vietnamese restaurant you took us to in that alley. We seldom get to mingle with the postmodern Parisian underclass.

You will, of course, be the star attraction.

Lyotard will be there also. We must humor him. You know what a colossal ego he has. I fear that the attention he's been getting from the Americans has made him lose his sense of proportion. Of course, he always had a tendency toward grandiosity.

The Americans have made you, Derrida, and Foucault into a minor academic industry. They lost Michel—how he loved to come to California and go to the leather bars—but they still have

you and Jacques, fortunately—and, of course,
Jean-François. Especially since your *Simulations*
came out, you've been very big in America. As
you've argued, American life is becoming increasingly more like Disneyland. Maybe the rest of
the world—even France—is going that way?

How curious it is, if you think about it,
that American intellectual life is so dominated
by the French. The French theorize. Then the
Americans explain the French theories and opera-
tionalize them, to some degree. In an endless
stream of books about what Baudrillard "really"
means...and whether you are undertheorized or
overtheorized.... I often wonder, if there were
no French theorists, and no Freud and no Marx
and no Saussure, what would the Americans do?
They'd be mute...except for the semioticians,
who could write about Peirce.

In any case, what I'd like you to discuss
in your lecture is, first, your work on material
culture as explicated in your *System of Objects*.
Give us more details about your theory that
we've created a hypercivilization and explain,
perhaps with your latest ideas, how the objects
we use function as signs that dominate our everyday lives in our societies of consumption. You
should explain your notions about the sign value
of objects, and your quite brilliant analysis of
the way objects confer prestige and indicate
power and status.

Your notions about our models being more
real than the manifestations based on them are
worth discussing. You suggest, for example, that
sex, as described in the sexual manuals, is more
ideal than the real thing and that the homes
described in the magazines are more ideal than
our actual homes. I hope you will give us your
latest thoughts on this subject.

Then, I'd like you to deal with your
theory of simulations and the new hyperreality.
You should talk about how computers and new

technologies have created a society based on signs and the codes that explain these signs, instead of the old society, based on manufacturing and the production of goods.

We live, you argue, in a society in which signs and simulations are more important than the things those signs and simulations stand for. In postmodern societies, the hyperreal simulations become more real than that which is simulated. We become hypnotized by the simulation and forget what is being simulated...perhaps like the movies, whose characters sometimes seem more real that we who watch them?

And you should point out how all this ends—how people then become "turned off," as we say here, become bored with the media and all the commercials that try to get them to do this and that, and then retreat into themselves and into an apathetic state. How did we get trapped in this image-dominated, hyperreal universe? Where do we find meaning? How do we escape from being captives of the media and the images they feed us? You must explain all this to the people who will be at the conference—as only you can do. Your book *America* has caused quite a stir in recent years. People will, no doubt, be asking you about it.

I've "signed you up" for this, to coin a joke.

There'll be a number of Americans speaking, also. I can't have a conference in America on postmodernism with only Frenchmen, Italians, and Germans, even though all we'll talk about are your theories and those of a few other Frenchmen, with an occasional Italian, German, or Russian thrown in to give the conference an international flavor. Jürgen Habermas, that "dour kraut" (as you well know), will be there, pushing his defense of modernism. You can demolish it at the conference—the way you've done elsewhere. Douglas Kellner, one of the best of the American postmodernists, and Fredric Jameson, of course, will be there. Also that Mark Poster fellow, from the University of California at Irvine. He's written a good book, *Existential Marxism in Postwar France*, and, more recently, edited a book of your essays. Lately, he seems to have gone crazy about computers. Like most American academics, he loves to hang around with Europeans. Do you think it's our accents? Or the conferences we have in Paris and Italy and nice places like that? There will also be some semioticians thrown into the mix. "Who steals my Peirce steals trash," I say.

In any case, you can expect to be attacked for being undertheorized by some, and for being overtheorized by others. Your friend Slavomir Propp will be speaking. He's helping me set up the conference. It's always good to have a linguist on hand; they have an innate sense of organization. He's gained a great deal of weight lately, and looks like a barn.

You remember Myra Prail, of course. I remember how you were taken with her. Well, she's still around, working as my research assistant. She's finishing her dissertation—doing it on postmodernism and capitalism. One of the people she's interested in, Basil Constant, is also helping me with the conference. So she's killing two birds with one stone, so to speak—helping me put on the conference and getting material for her dissertation. I'm trying to get her a job at Illinois, where they have an interest in literary theory. She wants to go to Irvine, but I don't know whether I can get her anything there.

Alain Fess is here for a year, also. I got him a grant. He's changed a good deal since he was my assistant. He never made it big in France, though his book was quite good. Unfortunately, he had an opening and didn't follow it up with anything. Now, I'm afraid, he sees himself as a failure and is a kind of corpse with

vital signs; he has resigned from life, though
he's still living. Maybe he'll come back to life
this year and stop just being a promising
scholar with one good book to his name. But it
takes discipline, and I'm afraid Alain doesn't
have enough of the work ethic.

Miyako Fuji is here, too. I know you've
been to a number of conferences with her.
Slavomir calls her a porcelain doll. She's quite
brilliant. I've been reading some of her work on
feminism lately. Very interesting. But she's
become somewhat strange. She seems to be acting
out Western fantasies of what Asian women are
like. Her hair is now very long, she wears translucent green makeup, and she dresses in rather
dramatic ways...sometimes in a postmodern,
almost punk, style. Then, at other times she
reverses things and goes native, if you know
what I mean. You never know what to expect from
her. She seems shy, but when you get to know
her, you discover that she's actually got a wry
sense of humor. Perhaps an absurdist sense of
humor is more accurate? And in her own quiet
way, she's very assertive. Strong women, who
keep doing unexpected things, can be dangerous.
You never know what absurdists are capable of
doing!

I've not been too well lately. Perhaps it's
from overwork? I went for a checkup several weeks
ago and the doctor was not too happy with the
results. I've got to see him next week, as a matter of fact. I've not said anything to Shoshana.
You know how worried she gets about anything.

You'll stay with us of, course. Jean-
François will be with us, also.

— *Ettore*

The goal of coming to an understanding [*Verstandigung*] is to bring about an agreement [*Einverstandnis*] that terminates in the intersubjective mutuality of reciprocal understanding, shared knowledge, mutual trust, and accord with one another. Agreement is based on recognition of the corresponding validity claims of comprehensibility, truth, truthfulness, and rightness. We can see that the term *understanding* is ambiguous. In its minimal meaning it indicates that two subjects understand a linguistic expression in the same way; its maximal meaning is that between the two there exists an accord concerning the rightness of an utterance in relation to a mutually recognized normative background. In addition, two participants in communication can come to an understanding about something in the world, and they can make their intentions understandable to one another.

Jürgen Habermas, *Communication and the Evolution of Society* (3).

chapter **twelve**

The third letter was to Jürgen Habermas.

March 11, 1996
Dear Jürgen:

I was greatly relieved to get your call the other day and find out that you'll be able to come to the conference on postmodernism we're having at Berkeley this summer. With you here, there will no doubt be a good dialectical argument at the conference. You will be the counterbalance to Jean-François Lyotard and Jean Baudrillard, my two French postmodernist propagandists. I suspect the real reason they're coming is so they can eat at Chez Panisse. That's the problem when we invite people to give lectures in Berkeley—they spend all their time at Chez Panisse or Masa's in San Francisco.

Is that a regression to modernist gastronomy? I hope you will be gracious enough to humor the two postmodernist "-ards." We could actually put them together into a Siamese-twin monster and create a postmodern, horrendous French beast, the Baudrillyotard. They have enormous egos and are incredibly full of themselves and the glory of French thought and culture, but, to give the devil his due, they have pushed the postmodernist argument forward. Or is it backward? Some would say the latter, and they may be correct.

And you, of course, will, in your classically rational way, return it to where it belongs. I'm looking for you to elaborate on your argument that postmodernist attacks on modernity stem from emotional and aesthetic attacks on Enlightenment rationality and are ultimately conservative...and, if pushed to their logical conclusions, end up in a reactionary form of protofascism. That's where incredulity toward meta-narratives and attacks on rational thinking and decision making lead, unfortunately.

Thus, your defense of modernity has enormous significance. For *you,* more than anyone else (I would argue), have understood the emancipatory potential and political implications of modernism. For it argues that people can function both as individuals and citizens, and, using rational thought, can criticize and ultimately help reform the political order. This possibility has not, alas, been realized yet. And that is because the multinational corporations have taken over, and, with their domination of the mass media, turned most individuals into relatively passive consumers of culture and spectators of mass-mediated spectacles, as you've argued for a number of years.

I agree with your argument that it is the ability of individuals to think, to reason, to criticize, to engage in rational discourse—and to find ways to resist cultural domination—that is our only hope. And this, of course, is a modernist agenda, one that sees humans as, whatever else we may be, sentient beings capable of rational thought. Of course, this capacity for reason has to be resurrected or reconstructed, given the aberrations in society caused by the

giant corporations. But this is possible. Here,
of course, your argument goes against that of
the postmodernists, who tend to privilege
emotion and irrationality and style.

I hope you will also talk about your belief
that there's been an important paradigm shift from
an era when consciousness was all-important to one
in which communication is now of major significance. The focus on consciousness, as you rightly
point out, leads to a privatistic sensibility,
a concern with self-preservation that distorts
rationality by focusing on its instrumental
consequences for individuals. *Communication,* as
you have suggested, leads in the other direction—
to *community* (the two words are allied, aren't
they?)—through the processes of discussion,
participation in society, and, with luck, consensus and agreement.

I expect that you and Jean-François will
have interesting things to say to one another?
Don't be too harsh on him. Now that he's become
a celebrity social theorist, he's spending more
time in front of the mirror (or so I understand)
than at the writing desk. Fredric Jameson will
also be giving a lecture; how could one have an
international conference on postmodernism without him? A moderate degree of argumentation, to
liven things up, would be nice, but no fisti-
cuffs (verbal, I mean) or anything too hot.

I've assembled a team to help me with the
details of the conference. You know how difficult it is to put these things on—having to
arrange transportation, housing, food, social
events, publicity, and so on takes an enormous
amount of time.

You'll love my research assistant Myra
Prail, who's been with me for the past few
years. She's got a Nordic beauty to her—blue
eyes, blond hair, perfect features, long legs,
breasts like Persian melons. She's also very

smart. She's doing some interesting work on the culture of capitalism and arguing, like Jameson, that contemporary American society is not post-modern but best described as at a particular stage of capitalism.

But don't be fooled. Underneath that lovely and innocent "American farm girl" exterior is, let me assure you, a shrewd and extremely calculating woman. She's very determined and disciplined. I pity anyone who gets in her way or blocks her view of the sun.

Alain Fess, a former student from a dozen or so years ago, is also here. If I recall correctly, you liked his book about American malls as quintessential expressions of postmodernism. He's still at the Centre National de la Recherche Scientifique in Paris. I got him a grant to come here, do some research, and help with the conference. Alain's biggest problem is that he's in the second or third rank of French intellectuals. He's good enough to be invited to some conferences here and there, but he's in the shadow of people like Baudrillard, Lyotard, and Foucault (may he rest in a peace that he never had in life). He did his doctorate with me; I had to work devilishly hard to get him through...and pull lots of strings, but for some reason he thinks I tried to prevent him from getting his degree.

For comedy, I have an English postmodernist novelist, Basil Constant, who sees himself as writing in the Calvino vein. He's written a number of novels, and a couple of them are pretty good. Oxford background and all that stuff, though I understand his father is what the British call a greengrocer. Of course you'd never know it, looking at Constant. He dresses as if he were the president of a university.

Slavomir is here. He's often at Berkeley. I think he has some kind of an arrangement that

allows him to teach at Moscow in the fall semester and at Berkeley during the spring semester.
He's grown enormously fat in recent years. Maybe
he's been spending too much time dining at
Postrio? In any case, he's as big as a Russian
bear. We think bears are cute in America—but
they actually are wild animals and very dangerous. I doubt that Slavomir is.

The last member of my team is a rather enigmatic Japanese woman, Miyako Fuji, from the University of Tokyo. It takes a bit of time to get used
to her. Sometimes she stares at people, and she
talks in a whisper most of the time. When she
relaxes, however, you find out that she's quite
normal. In a way, she's extremely beautiful. Propp
says she's a porcelain doll—hollow and without anything inside. That is, he thinks she's all mind
and cold logic, but I suspect that she's just the
opposite—volcanic and about to explode any time. I
assume that, like many Japanese, what she really
wants to do is to escape from Japan, that iron
cage of irrationality.

Shoshana is well and sends her love.

You'll stay with us, of course—unless you
prefer something more private. You'd have to have
breakfast with Lyotard and Baudrillard, who also
are staying with me. And if that is too much for
you to take, I can arrange something else.

— *Ettore*

The second feature of this list of postmodernisms is the effacement in it of some key boundaries or separations, most notably the erosion of the older distinction between high culture and so-called mass or popular culture. This is perhaps the most distressing development of all from an academic standpoint, which has traditionally had a vested interest in preserving a realm of high or elite culture against the surrounding environment of philistinism, of schlock and kitsch, of TV series and *Reader's Digest* culture, and in transmitting difficult and complex skills of reading, listening and seeing to its initiates.

Fredric Jameson,

"Postmodernism

and Consumer

Society" (112).

chapter **thirteen**

The fourth letter was to Fredric Jameson.

March 11, 1996
Dear Fred:

Thank you for your call and your letter. I'm delighted you'll be coming to the conference here in what some people call "The People's Republic of Berkeley." Is it solidarity with the proletarians of Berkeley that's the real reason you're coming here? Now that I know you'll be here, I'm confident there will be fireworks. After all, how many unreconstructed Marxists do we have around nowadays who can argue—and have their arguments taken seriously—that Marxism is the only meta-narrative that makes sense?

Credulity toward Marxism to counter the "incredulity toward meta-narratives" that your old friend Jean-François talks about...endlessly, so it seems. He's really cashed in on those three words and, thanks to them, is now at the later state of capitalism at which you find postmodernism. He'll be at the conference, of course.

You'll explain, I take it, your notion that reality in our state of late capitalism is now dominated by images and that our sense of

time, as something passing and leaving a historical record, has been changed. And that with time
fragmented and broken up, we all live now in a
succession of seemingly discontinuous presents.
I hope, also, that you'll expand on your argument about presentism and the way it corrodes
our sense of history and of the past. And your
notions of the way we experience history.

History, you assert, is not simply a narrative text but is tied, ultimately, to class
conflict. How do you answer those who suggest
we can only know history through texts, through
narratives? Also, you might offer some words on
your argument about the political situation in
America and the necessity of various small pro-
test groups here to form alliances to gain any
measure of power.

In a related matter, I hope you'll explain
the argument you made in your book *Postmodernism, or the Cultural Logic of Late Capitalism*
that what we call postmodernism is really a new
stage in the "cultural development of the logic
of late capitalism," a cultural dominant that
generates new forms of consciousness. It would
be helpful for you to discuss the way you period-
ize the development of capitalism and also to
explain how market capitalism generates realism,
how monopoly capitalism leads to modernism, and
how the era of multinationalist capitalism generates postmodernism. Thus postmodernism is not
based on a rupture with the past but instead is
part of the evolution of capitalism.

Will you be showing slides and talking
about the way the hyperspace in new hotels, like
the Bonaventure in Los Angeles, distorts our
sensoria? I hope you will also deal with the
attacks of your critics who argue that you don't
prove your hypotheses but merely assert them in
a kind of crude econo-cultural determinism, and
with those critics who suggest that your account

of postmodernism is undertheorized and is too
totalizing.

I was looking at your earlier book, *The
Prison-House of Language*, your discussion of
structuralism—the notion that texts can best be
understood when we focus upon the relationships
among elements in them—and Russian formalism,
and didn't see any mention in it of modernism
and postmodernism. It came out in 1972, so I
guess it took a while for you to start dealing
with postmodernism. That would be a good topic
to talk about, also. That is, *why* you started
writing about postmodernism.

Finally, you might dwell on some of the
subjects you deal with in your most excellent
introduction to Jean-François's *The Postmodern
Condition*. I'm sure people will be interested
in your comments about Lyotard's rejection of
Habermas's vision of a new type of communicational
society, based on rationality and your discussions
of the central importance of narratives.

Jean-François will be at the conference,
along with Baudrillard and Jürgen Habermas, as
well as various others—the collection of somewhat compulsive conference-goers with whom you
and I are so familiar. Is obsessive-compulsive
conference-going, supposedly a means of sharing
ideas and furthering knowledge, in reality just
a form of masochism, or is it a means of travel-
ing around at someone else's expense? Or all
of these?

In any case, Kazimierz Tigulski from Coper-
nicus University is coming. Is there a conference anywhere, on any subject, that he has not
attended? I've heard he's even managed to attend
two conferences, going on at the exact same
dates, in New York and New Delhi. Also Takahashi
Ikegama from Tokyo; Umberto Lombardino-Snitzlob
from Milano; Karl-Heinz Zeitwurst from Berlin;
Eeinno Risto Koiviisiitutto from Finland; Lucia

Santa-Maria Figueiredo from Brazil; Ripley Snell
from Amherst College; Father Clive Dilatus from
Notre Dame; Agostino Glioma from Berkeley;
Webster Civet from Oral Roberts University;
Alistair Hornbeam from Duke; Claudia Hip from
Barnard; LaVerne Palmetto from the University of
Miami; Charles Reed, Esquire, from Washington,
D.C.; Clarence Endive from Southwest Missouri
State University; Myron Goldfinger, the
postmodernist architect; the critic Clement Lard
and his lover Franco Bacon; A. Michael Noll from
Bell Labs; Sophia Craze from Sage Publications
in London; and the Israeli socio-semiotician
Danielihu Katz-Dayan...plus many others we've
seen again and again. Where they get their
travel funds is beyond me.

We're strapped for money here at the University of California, since the state's been in
the hole for ten billion dollars the last few
years. Of course, we do have enormous amounts of
money to pay our retiring presidents and other
administrators. And we'll have enough to take
you and the other main speakers out to dinner at
your favorite restaurants. You needn't worry
about going hungry in Berkeley.

I believe you know most of the people who
are helping me with the conference. Alain Fess,
a student of mine some ten years ago, is here.
He showed a lot of promise but never really did
anything after his first book. And so is
Slavomir Propp, who is now a much more substan-
tial figure than in earlier days. He's big
enough for two Propps—we could call them the
brothers Slavomir and Miroslav Propp. I think
he's become fat from going to so many
conferences to talk about postmodernism.

Do you remember Miyako Fuji, who ran that
wonderful conference in Tokyo? She's here. I'll
never forget the time she took a bunch of us out
to lunch in this rather ordinary-looking place,

and the bill for us was more than a thousand dollars. I guess the Japanese are used to such astronomical prices. She's become somewhat strange. Or, to be more precise, sometimes she acts strangely. She's often very intense. Other times, she's quite normal and very personable. I can't figure it out. Maybe she's on drugs or has some kind of a neurological condition? In any case, she's taken to dressing quite dramatically, with translucent Day-Glo lipsticks and green eyeshadow. The effect is quite striking.

There's also someone named Basil Constant, a British novelist who writes postmodern thrillers who's been with us for quite a while. He's got that Oxford polish...the school *does* do something for the students who go there. I'm not sure how they do it. You know these medieval institutions...they have something we've lost.

Finally, I've got a new research assistant, Myra Prail. She's the latest in a long line of brainy beauty queens who have been my assistants. The number of men who have killed themselves, or thought of killing themselves, over her is supposed to be quite enormous. She looks something like a more svelte Marilyn Monroe, but doesn't have Monroe's aura of innocence, vulnerability, and naiveté. She's also got Grace Kelly's coolness. Myra, I'm confident, will go far. She's quite determined...and possibly may be ruthless.

Shoshana sends her love. She's looking forward to seeing you again...and will make some rugelach for you. I believe it was the rugelach you liked so much on your last visit. We'll be more than happy to put you up—if you don't mind having breakfast with Lyotard, Baudrillard, and Habermas.

— Ettore

Simplifying to the extreme, I define *postmodern* as incredulity toward metanarratives. This incredulity is undoubtedly a product of progress in the sciences: but that progress in turn presupposes it. To the obsolescence of the metanarrative apparatus of legitimation corresponds, most notably, the crisis of metaphysical philosophy and of the university institution which in the past relied on it. The narrative function is losing its functors, its great hero, its great dangers, its great voyages, its great goal.

Jean-François Lyotard, *The Postmodern Condition: A Report on Knowledge* (xxiv).

chapter **fourteen**

"What a funny guy this Gnocchi was,"

thought Police Inspector Solomon Hunter, as he put the file of letters Ettore Gnocchi had written back into the filing cabinet. "I'll have copies made so I can study them in more detail, later." He looked around the office. In one of the bookcases he noticed a number of videotapes. He quickly read their labels. They were tapes of Gnocchi's lectures from his course on postmodernism.

He went to the living room, where everyone was sitting with stony faces.

"You may all go home," Hunter announced. "But you're not to leave town. I want you to come back to this house tomorrow morning at ten o'clock. If you aren't here, we'll get arrest warrants for you . . . and will make life quite uncomfortable. Any questions?"

"Do you have any idea who . . . who it was that killed Ettore?" asked Myra Prail.

"I've some ideas," said Hunter. "These kinds of crimes take time."

It was Hunter's style not to say very much. But his eyes caught little signs . . . nervous twitches on a person's face, subtle changes in skin color, beads of perspiration on someone's forehead. Long years of experience with criminals had taught him many things, and he had a kind of street savvy and intelligence that people often didn't recognize. Too many criminals had underestimated him, been put off by his rather casual manner, and later regretted having done so.

Everyone in the room got up and, with pained faces and downcast eyes, slowly filed out.

Hunter motioned to Sergeant Talcott Weems. "Come with me to the study. There's a video we should look at."

"Would you like some coffee? I'll be happy to make some for you," said Shoshana TelAviv.

"No thanks," said Hunter.

"What about you?" she asked Weems.

"Maybe later," said the sergeant.

The two policemen walked to Gnocchi's study.

"He's got videos of his lectures from the course on postmodernism he offered this term," said Hunter, pointing to a shelf full of videos. "What do you say we look at the last lecture he gave in his course on the subject?"

"Let's do it," said Weems. "Maybe we'll learn something interesting . . . if not about postmodernism, then about the late Professor Ettore Gnocchi."

America is neither dream nor reality. It is a hyperreality. It is a hyperreality because it is a utopia which has behaved from the very beginning as though it were already achieved. Everything here is real and pragmatic, and yet is the stuff of dreams too. It may be that the truth of America can only be seen by a European, since he alone will discover here the perfect simulacrum—that of the immanence and material transcription of all values. The Americans, for their part, have no sense of simulation. They are themselves simulation in its most developed state, but they have no language in which to describe it, since they themselves are the model. As a result, they are the ideal material for an analysis of all possible variants of the modern world. No more and no less in fact than were primitive societies in their day. The same mythical and analytic excitement that made us look towards those earlier societies today impels us to look in the direction of America. With the same passion and the same prejudices.

Jean Baudrillard,
America **(28–29).**

chapter **fifteen**

Hunter slipped the video out of its box

and placed it in the VCR. He pressed the play button and turned the television set to channel three. There was some grainy leader on the tape, but after a few seconds the figure of Ettore Gnocchi appeared on the screen. He was on the stage of a very large auditorium full of students who were applauding him.

"That's curious," said Weems. "They're applauding before he's given his lecture."

"He's already given a number of lectures. The students obviously liked him . . . or liked his lectures. Doesn't he look a bit different?"

"Video makes everyone look different," said Weems. "It's like photography. There's always a bit of a shock we feel when we see photos of ourselves. We look so different. But I see what you're talking about."

"Ladies and gentlemen, students, postmodernists . . .," said Gnocchi, raising both his hands in the air above his head and signaling for the students to stop clapping. "Thank you, thank you. If we can quiet down, I shall begin. This will be my last lecture in this course on postmodern theory . . . a lecture I trust you will find most interesting . . . and, like all the other lectures, perhaps even amusing."

"His last lecture," said Hunter. "He didn't realize that it really *would* be his last lecture. Ever."

Gnocchi had clipped a small microphone onto the lapel of his suit coat and started pacing back and forth. He had a bemused expression on his face—as if he knew the answer to some cosmic joke that the universe was playing on everyone, or that he was playing on everyone in the room . . . and the universe.

"We are, as I've suggested time and time again, prisoners of language, among other things. Remember that Lacan argued that the unconscious is structured like a language and language is what ultimately shapes the self, via relationships it establishes with others, and society. We see this when we consider the Internet . . . where people experiment with making and reconstructing their identities. In a sense we can say that society, working through language, helps us construct our selves. We are all inhabited, one might say, by the societies that have given us language. The notion that we exist, somehow, apart from society and the language it gives us, is an illusion.

"And likewise, we are prisoners of the classification systems we use, based upon language, to make sense of things. For example, and let me take something quite silly—suppose we have a man with no hair. Let me ask a question: Are men bald because they have no hair . . . or does the fact that we have no hair mean we're bald? Is baldness a condition? Or a description? Or neither?"

"What kind of nonsense is this?" asked Weems. "Is this what parents pay thousands of dollars in tuition for? Is that what it means to go to Berkeley?" He scratched his head reflexively, wondering if he were balding too fast.

On the videotape, Gnocchi continued speaking. "Supposing we see before us a man with a thick head of hair. Then he grabs hold of his hair and lifts it, revealing a head without any hair on it. If we didn't see him reveal that he was wearing a wig, is it fair to say that the man is bald? And then there's the matter of degree. When is a man bald? At what point do we say he's bald—when there's thinning at some spot on his scalp? When there's the first spot without hair on his scalp? Or when there's more scalp revealed than hair? Or when there's no hair at all? Suppose a man develops baldness from the front. How far back does his hair have to retreat for him to be bald? What about a person who has a full head of hair but shaves it off—like some basketball players have done. They have no hair, but are they bald? No. Being bald suggests an inability to have a full head of hair, and is not the same thing as not having any hair because of style preferences.

"There is also the matter of identity. How much of our identity is connected with our having a full head of hair or our being bald? And why does baldness *matter* so much? Are we the same person when we have a full head of hair as we are when we don't have a hair on our head, because shaving off all one's hair is, for the moment, fashionable? Or if we don't have much hair because we are bald? If not, why? And when our hair turns gray, are we different in any significant way?

"Suppose we gain ten pounds. Are we much different? What about twenty pounds? People say, 'He's put on a bit of weight' or 'He's getting fat.' But aren't we the same person? Or are we?"

Gnocchi paused and glanced around the lecture hall. "The only method of freeing learning, at once, from these abstruse questions, is to enquire seriously into the nature of human understanding, and show, from an exact analysis of its powers and capacity, that it is by no means fitted for such remote and abstruse subjects."

"He raises some interesting questions about identity," said Hunter. "From what I gather, postmodern thinkers are obsessed with this matter . . . because they see contemporary society as being dominated by images and imitations of things. What one of them, a French thinker named Baudrillard, calls 'simulations.' "

"Strikes me as really moronic," replied Weems.

"How do we maintain our identities," Gnocchi continued, "in the face of constant change? Especially in a society when everything, if the Marxists and postmodernists are correct, is reduced to commodification. When we are all commodities, who create our identities through what we consume, and who sell ourselves, one way or another, reflecting our alienation, generally to the highest bidder."

Hunter grabbed the remote control and put the VCR on freeze frame.

"I'll be damned," he said. "Gnocchi seems . . . I can't quite figure it out . . . different, somehow. He looks the same but he also looks different, somehow."

"Maybe if he had a bullet hole in the middle of his forehead and a dart sticking out of his cheek and a knife in his back, he'd look like he did when we found him?" said Weems. "Once the spark of life leaves a person, they look different, somehow. They're dead matter, and their faces generally take on a peaceful look. Remember his face? He almost seemed to be smiling, as he was lying there dead with his head on his own dining table. I don't know much about this postmodernism stuff, but it strikes me as utter nonsense. As *absurd*. Is that what we pay professors at Berkeley to do—speculate about whether men who have no hair are

bald or whether they're bald because they have no hair?! I say it's a
lot of baloney. Ridiculous."

Hunter clicked the play button on the remote control and
the video resumed playing.

"Now, this matter of anxiety about baldness in males is, of
course, quite ridiculous," continued Gnocchi.

"Looks like he heard you, Talcott," said Hunter with a
chuckle, then turned to watch the TV screen.

"It's a socially induced panic. We are not born with
concerns about whether we have hair or not when we are older;
rather, we learn it, and we learn it indirectly—from the media,
from the insidious simulations that occupy so much of our time
and, without our recognizing it, shape our personalities and our
desire system. We see countless commercials in which young,
good-looking men and beautiful women are paired together. We
seldom see commercials in which old bald men—like myself, for
example—are paired with gorgeous young women. Or gorgeous
young bald women paired with older men with full manes."

The students in the class laughed, the sound echoing
throughout the auditorium.

"Sexuality and desire are now commodities, linked to other
commodities. Our lives are, all too often, empty, hollow things,
filled up with meaningless work, for the most part, and anxiety
about being fired, if we are fortunate enough to have work. And
our leisure hours are filled up with time wasted, all too often sitting in front of a television set. The great philosopher, Berkeley,
said, 'To be is to be perceived.' I would update that notion now
and say 'To be is to be seen on television.' Thus, the world we live
in now, the postmodern world, is divided between those who are
on television, who are seen, who are somebodies, and everyone

else—those who are not on television, who are not seen, those who are nobodies. These nobodies gaze, stupidly and endlessly, in some kind of a dreamlike trance, at the somebodies who are on the media, at the images that flash before them, at the simulacra.

"We've developed an occulocentric, or vision-centered, society, in which seeing is more important than being, than participating in society, than doing things with others. We know that people often prefer to see things on television that they could see with their own eyes if they looked out the window. A parade is passing by, down the street on which you live. Do you look out the window and see the real parade, or do you watch the parade on television? The simulation, the dancing dots that form images, have a greater reality for most of us than the real thing. If you watch the real parade, you'll miss the commentary from the experts that tells you how to think about the parade, commentary that gives you background information, and the various close-ups and exciting camera shots that give the parade a spurious kind of vitality. Reality and the image are merging, which forces us to consider the matter of representation and that which is real or original."

Gnocchi stopped lecturing for a moment to gaze about the room, massaged both temples with his forefingers, then resumed. "Life, like many films, is becoming a remake—of our own lives, of our fantasies about what our lives might possibly be, or, in more and more cases, of someone *else's* life. We end up, in too many cases, leading someone else's life . . . or imitating it as best we can. Life has become theater and our lives are more and more looking like not the 'real thing' but performances."

"He's really getting excited here," said Weems. "He's pacing back and forth and has really become animated. I can see why he might be a popular teacher, though I still find his ideas a bit curious."

"I find what he's saying very interesting," said Hunter. "Are we seeing what Gnocchi called 'the real thing' with the people involved in this case, or are we seeing very clever performances by a cast of ingenious actors and actresses? It's hard to say."

"In this make-believe world," Gnocchi added, "everything collapses into itself and all boundaries are broken. An opera on television and a soap opera on television become almost the same thing—two examples of mass-mediated culture, and many postmodernists would argue, to generalize the point, that there's no significant difference between elite arts (like opera and ballet) and popular arts (like situation comedies and commercials). Everything becomes blurred. We now prize put-ons, irony, eclecticism, and mixing genres and everything else up. We construct buildings using five different architectural styles. We worship together not in churches but in shopping malls; we get married not in cathedrals but in drive-through chapels on the Las Vegas strip. We give increased status to mediated images while we attack traditional literary and artistic canons for being irrelevant, old-fashioned, and bourgeois. It is television, along with popular music forms, and the cinema now that give us 'our' ideas about class, about sexuality, about gender formations, about ethnicity, about politics, about ideology, about race, about roles and status—about *everything*."

Professor Gnocchi paused again for emphasis. "And television and the media generate self-hatred and alienation in those who are not able to afford the lifestyle projected by the television shows and films we watch. This self-hatred leads to alienation and a desire for revenge, a desire some people have, as they feel themselves sinking, to pull down everything and everyone in society with them. We hate ourselves (even if we aren't conscious of this and often can't articulate these feelings), and then we project our self-hatred onto others, especially those who are not like us—gays, women, African-Americans, Jews, members of other ethnic and racial minorities, foreigners.

"The period from after the Second World War to the present is the one that has been described as the time when postmodernism triumphed, though, as I've pointed out earlier, some theorists argue that we aren't living in a postmodern age but one best described as 'late modernism.' Jameson has argued that the postmodern era is best understood as being the third stage of capitalism, an era shaped by what he calls the 'cultural logic of late capitalism.' And capitalism, many theorists suggest, generates what might be termed a culture of capitalism.

"Jameson argues that we've moved from the first stage, market capitalism, when realism was the cultural dominant, to the second stage, monopoly capitalism, when modernism was dominant in the culture, to a third, late stage, multinational capitalism—and the dominant cultural style of this stage is postmodernism. Cultural development can be seen then as a by-product, so to speak, of the economic system that shapes our consciousness, and by doing that, shapes the institutions we create in society. Jameson believes that Marxism, the last great meta-narrative of the twentieth century, is not irrelevant and not something to be dismissed. In the final analysis, a Marxist position would suggest that the hidden theme running through postmodernist styles and cultural forms is that of ideological domination by the ruling classes.

"But precisely *how* our multinational stage of capitalism generates the postmodern culture it does is not quite clear. Yes, the commodification of culture generates the shopping mall and our consumer culture, aided and abetted by the advertising industry, which colonizes our desire. But how do you explain the counterculture movements, the increased power of marginal groups like gays and lesbians and ethnic minorities? Traditional Marxists argue that these groups are tolerated here in America because they give people the illusion that America is a democratic country and that everyone is free to live life as he or she wishes . . . the illusion that we are all free to realize the American dream of success through hard work because opportunity is available. But—"

Gnocchi suddenly stopped. His face turned bright red and he started gasping for breath. He walked back to the lectern, haltingly, took a pill from a small plastic bottle he was carrying in his pocket, and took a drink of water.

"What do you make of that?" asked Hunter. "Gnocchi seems to have had some kind of an attack. Doesn't look like heart trouble, though you never can tell. . . . Obviously he's got some kind of a serious medical problem. Maybe with his respiratory system, with his breathing? Looks like it might be an asthma attack."

"I'll check into this tomorrow. I'll get in touch with his doctor," answered Weems. "And I'll see what the autopsy reveals."

After a minute or two, Gnocchi seemed to have caught his breath and resumed lecturing.

"Please forgive me," he said to the students. "I've not been too well, lately. But my doctor told me not to worry and I'm taking him at his word."

Hunter clicked the pause button on the remote control to halt the video for a moment.

"He didn't give anything away, did he?" said Weems.

"No," Hunter replied, getting a little worried about the case. "At least not verbally. I'm going to have a copy made of this video and have the station's medical experts take a look at it. There are two reasons why a doctor might tell a patient not to worry. One is because the patient is in good health and has minor problems. And the other because the patient is seriously ill and beyond help."

"It didn't matter which it was," said Weems, "since Gnocchi was murdered."

"Let's look at a bit more of the video," Hunter suggested. He pressed the play button and the videotape continued playing.

"Let me resume," Gnocchi said. "Guided by images we carry in our personal and collective consciousness, from television programs and films and other media experiences, some people, who go crazy, become what I call 'Terminators.'"

Gnocchi went to a table on the platform, turned on a VCR, and put a videocassette in it. He played a couple of minutes from the action movie *The Terminator*; it flashed on the screens of half a dozen large monitors that were on metal frames attached to the walls in various places in the lecture hall. He showed the scene in which the Terminator is using a submachine gun to blast away a police station. After a few minutes, Gnocchi turned off the VCR.

"Armed with submachine guns and other weapons," he declared, "like Arnold Schwarzenegger in *The Terminator*, these modern-day Terminators, their submachine guns blazing, destroy those they hate . . . or those whose destruction will cause the most grief to those they hate. And they destroy themselves, too. But even though they may die, these crazed Terminators do manage to escape from that radical anonymity in which they were imprisoned, as they have their photos flashed across innumerable television screens and reprinted in newspapers all across the country, and sometimes the world.

"Yes, you were a nobody before you seized your automatic pistols and submachine guns and butchered people, and now, all of a sudden, you've made headlines all over the world and you've been seen in every town that television reaches, in every corner of the globe. In a bizarre way, using debased logic, terrorists and killers become famous and, in a perverted way, achieve a kind of heroic status; if you can't be a hero, they seem to believe, be a world-class anti-hero—but be *sure* you make headlines around the world and get your picture on the national news programs and on CNN and, lately, the Internet. You may be imprisoned or even executed, but you'll have made your presence known and will not go to your grave as a nobody, like most of the people you know.

"After your death," the professor continued, "people will start fighting with one another when they try to explain your behavior. Some will say you were crazy. It will be discovered, perhaps, that you were a loner who loved guns and finally something happened, the notorious straw that broke the camel's back, and you went crazy. Since you had guns, you killed people; simple. Others will say something's wrong with American society and culture, and blame the media for being too violent, blame American culture for having a history of violence, and blame the government. Maybe you were connected to some organization, or believed fervently in some cause . . . you might have been allied with the right-wing militias or some left-wing group, or perhaps the right-to-life movement. Whatever the case, your organization will be blamed for using people like you, people who were susceptible to being manipulated, people who believed that it was morally correct—even if they had to sacrifice their lives—to kill people in the name of a great cause, in the name of some meta-narrative.

"In three days' time, however, you'll have been forgotten, as the next atrocity is committed and the next person, fighting his or her—though it almost always is *his*—sense of estrangement,

alienation, and radical anonymity, takes up his rifles and submachine guns, looking for his fifteen minutes of fame that, so Andy
Warhol suggested, is allotted to everyone. Were each person to get
fifteen minutes of fame, maybe the people who become Terminators would not feel the need to take up their guns? Or, for the
more cowardly ones, bombs."

Again Gnocchi paused, to take a deep breath and adjust
the microphone clipped to his lapel. "We see, then, that American
society—the most postmodern society extant (or so the French
theorists tell us)—has now lost its coherence, is no longer unified.
Just like the buildings created by postmodernist architects that use
many different styles, American society is now a crazy mixture of
microsocieties, of subcultures, at war in many respects with one
another, that lead to our lives, all too often, being what Hobbes
said they would be—'nasty, brutish, and short.'

"And now, in the best postmodernist tradition, I become a
video disk jockey and offer another example of postmodernist
entertainment . . . a few minutes of a music video by Laurie
Anderson."

He went over to the lectern and got another videocassette.
Then he put the video into the VCR on the podium.

"Let's watch some of Laurie Anderson's 'Oh, Superman.' "
A few students started to clap, then checked their impulse.

When the song finished, he turned off the videocassette
player and resumed his lecture.

"We no longer believe in meta-narratives, in overarching
systems of belief and thought. We no longer are sure of how institutions gain legitimacy. We no longer can separate the image from
reality, leading to a so-called crisis of representation. We search,
endlessly, for meaning in films, television programs, novels, and
other works—and for hidden ideologies that may be shaping our

consciousness. In addition, we see ourselves as existing in states of radical alienation, our lives turned into commodities, our lives characterized by stylistic eclecticism and promiscuity, with the media shaping our consciousness. What we are looking for is a means of resisting, a means of connecting with the past but not being enslaved by it, a means of helping the dispossessed gain a measure of autonomy and self-respect.

"Maybe we are all waiting for Superman to rescue us—but you and I know that he won't because there *is* no Superman. Not really. So it is to *you,* the younger generation," he said, pointing to the students, "it is to *you* that we turn, for you are our only hope. It is only your generation—immunized, ironically, by your over-exposure to the media—it is only your generation that can save us . . . that *must* save us. It is you who must resist, you who must help us establish community again, you who must help us regain our societies and, with them, our identities and our lives. I hope you will rise to the occasion." Gnocchi let his words hang in the air for a moment, then said, "Thank you" and unclipped his lapel microphone and wiped his brow with a handkerchief.

The students started applauding. Several in the front of the auditorium stood up, and they were joined by others until the whole class was standing, clapping loudly and cheering. Several of them started chanting Gnocchi's name.

"Gnoc-chi! Gnoc-chi! Gnoc-chi!" they shouted, clapping and cheering. Ettore Gnocchi blew kisses to everyone. The tape ended and the television monitor the policemen were looking at showed only static.

"They really loved the guy, didn't they?" said Weems, puzzled. "I must admit, I don't get all this postmodernism stuff, but his students seem to have really taken to it. And to him. Of course they had a semester with him, and we don't know what his other lectures were like."

"Yes," said Hunter. "A remarkable performance. Really remarkable. He had quite a, what should I call it? . . . quite a brilliant stage presence. But isn't that what, in large part, post-modernism is about? Maybe, when you get to the heart of the matter, when you scratch beneath the surface, all these post-modernists are really performance artists? Postmodernists celebrate the surface, say that truth is not unitary but always contingent and provisional, and focus on the media, computers, and technology. Well . . . how much difference is there between Gnocchi's lecture and that video by Laurie Anderson he played? Gnocchi didn't use musical instruments and synthesizers, but he's more like her and some of the other performance artists that I've read about in the *San Francisco Chronicle* than he is a conventional professor."

"I think it was his *style* of saying things more than what he said that is basic," replied the sergeant. "Gnocchi had no interest in the functionality of our institutions—no concern, it would seem, about how systems in society interrelate and help maintain society. To me, postmodernism seems to be an excuse for people who are on the margins, who don't believe in consensus . . . or anything much, so it appears. I found his ideas distasteful, though his passion came through and the students felt it. No doubt about that.

"But this business about incredulity toward meta-narratives," Weems went on, "about not accepting any grand theories or belief systems, about a multiperspectivist frame of reference . . . I don't think the postmodernists are right about this. If a robber were to steal something from a postmodernist, he'd be on the phone to the police quick as a wink. It's like doctors. People complain about doctors . . . until they get sick, that is . . . and then it's off to see one. *If* they can get an appointment, that is."

"I'm not so sure you're right," said Hunter. "When you get a chance to read some of Gnocchi's letters, as I did a little while ago, you'll have a better notion of what postmodernism is than you do now. Believe me, Talcott. You can't understand postmodernism or judge everything by Gnocchi's lecture."

The term "*post*modernity" indicates what comes after modernity. Modernity may be traced to the Renaissance, developed during the Age of Enlightenment, and coming to full bloom by the time of the French Revolution. Modernity places man in the centre, and sees man as a rational being. There is a basic assumption of emancipation and progress through reason and science. . . . It is debatable whether postmodernity is actually a break with modernity, or merely its continuation. Postmodern writers may prefer to write history so that their own ideas appear radically new. Postmodern themes were present in the romanticism of the last century, in Nietzsche's philosophy at the turn of the century, with the surrealists in literature, for instance in Bliven and Borges. What is new today is the pervasiveness of postmodern themes in culture at large.

Steinar Kvale,

"Postmodern

Psychology:

A Contradiction

in Terms?" (32).

chapter **sixteen**

Shoshana TelAviv couldn't fall asleep

until very late that evening, restlessly tossing and turning until it was three o'clock in the morning. The events of the past evening had shocked her. First she had felt numb—the way you feel after you hear some terrible news. And then she started crying. She thought having something to eat might soothe her but she wasn't hungry.

After she had put the food away and cleaned up, she tried reading, but her mind kept racing, returning to Ettore's horrible death. She couldn't hold back the tears, so she had a small glass of Scotch. The police had swarmed all over the house, taking endless numbers of photographs, looking at everything. She didn't know what they were looking for, or what they found.

When she finally did manage to fall asleep she had a very strange dream.

I was on a streetcar in some city . . . it might have been in Europe? Maybe Prague or Istanbul? Perhaps Copenhagen? Or Gothenburg? It was an old streetcar, I recall. . . . It looked as if it had been manufactured in the early 1900s. It most certainly had seen better days. It needed painting and the seats needed varnishing. Its route took it through one of the meaner sections of the city. Hardly anyone was on the streets . . . which were full of rubbish, broken pieces of furniture, and garbage. Wild dogs wandered around in packs. Many of the stores were empty; others were boarded up. I did see some people sitting in coffee shops and bars. Some drunks were lying on the sidewalk, here and there. I was with someone . . . a man who was disabled and could only move by using crutches. It was painful to see him. We were at the back of the streetcar. It was around eight o'clock. We had just had dinner at a very fine restaurant—full of sparkling crystal glasses and obsequious waiters. My friend and I made small talk as we dined on lobsters and white wine. "I like the simple things in life," he said, as he popped a piece of lobster into his mouth. If I recall correctly, he was a wealthy banker . . . something like that. We left the restaurant and boarded a streetcar. It was crowded with rough and crude-looking people. They looked faintly menacing. Many of them, the ones who had seats, were sitting with their eyes closed . . . or even sleeping. Their clothes were ragged and they smelled of garlic. In the front of the streetcar, a man was yelling that Christ was coming . . . in German . . . or was it Dutch? "All sinners had better prepare to meet their end!" he screamed. Nobody paid attention to him. We were on our way to a lecture . . . or was it a play? Perhaps a recital? Now that I think of it, I believe it was a concert of chamber music. Whatever the case, the streetcar seemed to stop every two hundred feet to let passengers off or take on new ones. The passengers all seemed to want to get off from the front of the streetcar or get on from the front, so there were an endless number of delays. "Let the passengers off, let them off!" the conductor would cry. The people would leave and then there would be a surge of bodies onto the streetcar.

"Please move to the back of the car," the conductor would shout. I can remember glancing at my watch, all the time . . . I was afraid we'd miss the opening piece. My companion said, "It looks like we'll be late. We should have taken a cab." He kept shifting his body on his crutches to make himself comfortable. There were no empty seats. Finally we arrived at our destination. It took my friend a long time to get off the street-car. I held his crutches while he maneuvered himself down the steps. When we were out of the streetcar we crossed the tracks and made it to the sidewalk. We had to walk over the bodies of drunken men and women who were scattered here and there on the sidewalk. Half a block down the street we could see the auditorium where we were going . . . a large, white baroque building that glistened brilliantly as searchlights played upon it. There was a mob of people in front. "We'll never get to our seats in time," I thought. My friend said he knew of a secret passage to the auditorium, in a building across the street, but I didn't wish to bother. Besides, the people were swarming into the building, so we decided to use the main entrance. The ticket takers were blind hunch-backs . . . who took our tickets, tore them in half, and cautioned us, "Hurry, hurry . . . you'll be late." We started racing down the central aisle in a mild panic. . . . I noticed that the back of the auditorium was quite empty . . . only a few people scattered here and there. But when we got to the front of the auditorium, people were looking for their seats. People who had sat down had to stand and let them by. I noticed that there were only men in the audience. "That's curious," I thought. We finally made it to our seats. After I sat down, I looked behind me. Every-one in the auditorium looked exactly the same—they all looked like Ettore! And they all had the same puzzled expression on their faces, one that seemed to say, "How could you *do* that?!" At that moment, the house lights started dimming to let us know the performance was about to begin. And then, suddenly . . . they turned off . . . the lights! The lights. . . .

With that, Shoshana awoke from her sleep, with a start. "My God," she thought, "what a horrible dream. What could it mean? That look on Ettore's face . . . what did it mean? What did he *know*?" She took a little notebook that she kept beside her bed and wrote it down.

Then, after she had stretched her limbs a moment and plumped her pillows, she sat up in bed and speculated in her notebook about the dream she had just had. "Postmodernism," she wrote, in her precise hand, "effaces the boundaries between popular culture and elite culture and between art and everyday life, between the waking state and the dream state. Curious how this dream reflects a postmodern sensibility. Has postmodernism started shaping our dreams? But why not? Or does postmodernism reflect our dreams? An interesting question.

"I can see the postmodernism reflected in my dream's Kafkaesque qualities, in its evocation of sites of cultural disorder such as the hall I went to in the dream, in its diffusive and subtly allegorical nature, in its labyrinthine themes—almost like one of Borges's stories, if you think about it. The dichotomy between fantasy and reality has been breached in my dream, just as it has been breached in the postmodern world, and it's hard to be sure that we're not sleeping—and merely *dreaming* that we're awake—a good deal of the time. That dream reminded me, in its narrative line, somewhat of MTV, a classic postmodernist genre, or maybe of all those grotesques of certain stylistic elements that were found in *Max Headroom*? Bizarre. But also terrifying and unsettling."

After she finished writing in her notebook, exhausted, she feel back asleep.

A collectivity that takes narrative as its key form of competence has no need to remember its past. It finds the raw material for its social bond not only in the meaning of the narratives it recounts, but also in the act of reciting them. The narratives' reference may seem to belong to the past, but in reality it is always contemporaneous with the act of recitation. . . . Narratives, as we have seen, determine criteria of competence and/or illustrate how they are to be applied. They thus define what has the right to be said and done in the culture in question, and since they are themselves a part of that culture, they are legitimated by the simple fact that they do what they do.

Jean-François Lyotard, *The Postmodern Condition: A Report on Knowledge* (22–23).

chapter **seventeen**

As was his custom, Alain Fess wrote in his journal

when he returned from his evening at the home of Ettore Gnocchi. He kept his journal in bound books and used it to speculate about things, consider articles and books he might write, and record his thoughts and events of significance.

> What an evening . . . the most horrendous I've ever had. For it seems that Ettore Gnocchi has been murdered while we were all sitting around the dinner table, chatting about the postmodernism conference. The lights went out, caused by a storm, no doubt . . . and when they went on again, Ettore was dead. He had a bullet hole in his head and a knife in his back and a dart with poison on it, surely, sticking out of his cheek. And most likely his drink was poisoned. We have a matter of considerable overdetermination here. He was killed too many ways at the same time. It doesn't make sense.
>
> Then a detective came with a collection of policemen who scoured the house looking for clues and that kind of thing . . . just like in detective novels. This was followed by a private interrogation of each of us by an inspector, one Solomon Hunter. He asked me whether I had any

notions about who might have wanted to kill Ettore and he asked about all the other people at dinner—Basil Constant, Shoshana TelAviv, Slavomir Propp, Myra Prail, and Miyako Fuji. He wanted to know who was sleeping with whom, how we all got along, what postmodernism is.

I can't tell whether he's an oaf or a rather sly and clever fellow. I suspect it's the latter. He has a look on his face that makes me think he knows more than he lets on. I suspect he's a very dangerous individual.

In any case, I told him what I knew. Then I had to wait around in the living room, with everyone else, while Hunter called each of us into Ettore's study and questioned us. It was most unpleasant . . . somewhat humiliating, as a matter of fact. We were all in a state of shock, so nobody said very much, except for small talk and that kind of thing. A police sergeant, someone named Weems, was with us and that prevented us from saying very much.

Shoshana is taking it very hard. Poor woman. How my heart goes out to her. She had a hard life with Ettore. He wasn't easy to live with and he wasn't very affectionate to her . . . perhaps because he had so many other interests, shall we say? Ettore always had beautiful young women as his research assistants, and we know how dirty old men can get their way, all too often, with impressionable young students. I don't know how Shoshana put up with him for so long. She's actually still quite a beautiful woman, too. She must have been absolutely gorgeous when she was younger. She seems to be involved with that gross Slavomir Propp. What she sees in that disgusting tub of lard is beyond me.

For some reason Hunter was interested in postmodernism and kept asking me about it. I told him it's impossible to explain it in a short conversation. I imagine he believes it has something to do with Ettore's murder? In any case, I told him about some of the basic ideas. If he read my book, *The Minotaur in the Shopping Mall,* he'd find out about post-modernism soon enough.

We have to go back to Ettore's house tomorrow morning, for some reason. Maybe this Hunter will have solved the crime by then? Who could have done it? And how did they do it? I had great respect for Ettore and I thought all of the others did, as well. But it seems that wasn't the case. I know that Ettore, according to Propp, had stolen his ideas. So Propp had a motive, possibly. But who else?

I'm so tired it's hard to know what to think. I'll have to get some sleep. I've not been sleeping well lately. Don't know why. Maybe the strain of helping to put on this conference and the thought of having to look after all the pompous asses that Ettore invited—Baudrillard, Lyotard, Jameson, Habermas . . . one's worse than the next. Of course working with Ettore is pure hell. People think he's charming and very amusing, but he's really a madman. Paranoid as hell and polymorphously perverse.

And when they're here, these postmodernist philosophers all want us to get girls for them—except the ones who want young boys, that is—and they all expect to be taken out to eat in expensive restaurants. Now that I think about it, I'm tired of conferences . . . even the ones I'm asked to speak at. For some reason it's been a while since I was asked to speak at a conference. Maybe I've got to develop some new material, write another book? But it's hard to follow a book like mine. You can't make major breakthroughs in thought all the time. I've got to have some time to rest and figure out my next move.

Sometimes I think my problem is that I have many talents but I lack the most important one—which is the ability to do something with whatever talents I may have. I seem to want to jump on a horse and ride off in all directions at the same time. I'm restless and can't seem to concentrate. Now that Ettore is dead, I won't have to worry about the conference . . . or so I imagine. Of course it's always possible that Shosh-ana will take the torch from Ettore, so to speak, but she's easy to deal with. It's terribly difficult to work with someone who's been your teacher; you never quite feel at ease, never feel comfortable about him. I know that's the way I felt about Ettore. . . .

Of course, people who weren't his students also had problems with him. He was hard to talk to. We'd be taking a walk and I'd be trying to carry on a conversation with him and he seemed to be lost in his thoughts, just connecting with me from time to time, when he felt like it. He was probably thinking about some new article or some new book . . . or some new graduate student who caught his eye. When Myra Prail leaves, he's got to find someone else. He never has male research assistants. Of course, who can blame him? Having a beautiful woman around to help one makes life much more enjoyable.

What am I saying?! The poor man's dead now. Even if he was a brute, it still is terrible what happened to him.

I wonder about Myra Prail? What would a young woman like that see in a nasty old man like Ettore? Young women like Myra may be OK for a short liaison . . . I could see that. But different generations don't mix well, and May–September relationships with graduate students never work out well. They're too problematic. . . . How do you keep your wife from finding out? And then how do you get rid of them when you're tired of them?

They graduate! Of course . . . then it's on to the next one. He had it all worked out. Leave it to Ettore to be practical about affairs of the heart (and genitals).

Now that he's dead, what will happen to Shoshana? I always wondered how she put up with him. Shoshana is really a beautiful woman, but in a way quite different from Myra. Shoshana is like a ripe peach— natural, sweet. . . . She's luminous, radiant. I wonder whether I'm in love with her? I think of her all the time. But I don't think of her quite the same way I think about Myra Prail—not at all.

I think of Shoshana as . . . as like a goddess . . . while I think of Myra Prail simply as the object of my priapic lust. I envy Ettore and his ability to have young women like Myra. He's a role model, in a sense . . . he shows that older men need not abandon their fantasies of having sex with juicy young women.

God, what am I thinking? No wonder I don't do any serious work anymore—all I do is think about sex all the time. Maybe I should go back to Miyako. I'm sure that she's still in love with me . . . and she's gorgeous, too. But she's become so icy, so cold. I don't know what happened to her. I'd better not call her . . . I don't want to start with her all over again. It might not be so easy to extricate myself. She's a spider and I don't want to get caught in her web again. That I escaped from her before was, I've always thought, a minor miracle.

I often wonder about Asian women . . . what are they thinking? Ridiculous, of course . . . they're just like all other women. My Aunt Josie always said "Women are women. We're all the same, when you get down to it." Josie, poor thing, was married to that monster Jean-Marie. . . . Every time I think of her I think of him and every time I think of him it reminds me of when I was hiking in Glion sur Montreux and stopped in an inn . . . the cook there was named Jean-Marie. . . . He made the most wonderful omelettes . . . I often wonder: were his omelettes better than the ones I had when I spent a summer in Grasse, and used to go to that little café there, on the outskirts of the city? The cook there was named Pascal . . . or was it Hubert? I keep forgetting. I must be losing my mind.

I remember I was supposed to give a lecture and a group of us went to Pascal's Café. There were four of us and we had a lovely lunch of omelettes and a salad and some cheesecake for dessert. And four bottles of wine—two of white and two of red. I was in a state of sheer terror when we drove back, through winding roads, but we made it . . . though I can't remember what happened after that. I must have given my lecture. Afterwards I remember I met this woman, Sophie. She was from Bagneres de Bigorre, if I recall. . . . We made love that night.

Sophie was a mathematician, from Paris X. I don't know what she was doing in Grasse. . . . She said she usually spent her holidays in Normandy but decided on something different. Actually, she may not have been a mathematician but a statistician. I know it had something to do with numbers. I always get mixed up. I mean, what is the difference between mathematics and statistics? Josie's husband, Jean-Marie, was an accountant, now that I think of it. He was good with figures . . . but not his own. He must have weighed 150 kilos. I wonder what happened to Sophie? She had the most beautiful teeth. White and pearly . . . that reminds me . . . I've got to make an appointment with the dentist.

After he finished writing in his journal, Alain Fess had a glass of wine, brushed his teeth, and went to bed. He looked over his journal.

"Hmm," he thought, "the contours of my latest entry in my journal are most interesting. My narrative could almost be something by Pynchon or Barthelme, in its reflection of a kind of dissociated and even alienated sensibility, in the way it jumps around from one thing to another, always going off on tangents, in its randomness, superficiality, and depthlessness.

"I seem, in this entry—and most of my other entries, now that I think about it—to be preoccupied with sex and food. What's so strange about that? Even postmodernists have to eat and take care of their sexual needs. This writing I did tonight: it does have the fissiparous, pastichelike quality that is so characteristic of postmodernity, shown in a linear manner instead of the all-at-onceness of, say, a work of visual art. Is not my time in Grasse paradigmatic of the postmodern emphasis on the carnivalesque, on tourism and places like theme parks, malls, and resorts as central aspects of postmodern cultural and social life? I've done the definitive work on malls in my book on the mall in Minnesota. What next? Maybe cruises would be a good subject? Excellent food, lots of women around. And you get to visit all kinds of exotic places. Very postmodern. Something to think about. I might be able to get a grant and spend a couple of years analyzing cruises."

Alain Fess turned out the light and immediately fell into a deep sleep. . . .

One postmodernist trope is the list, as if culture were a garage sale, so it is appropriate to evoke postmodernism by offering a list of examples, for better and for worse: Michael Graves' Portland Building, Philip Johnson's AT&T, and hundreds of more or less skillful derivatives; Robert Rauschenberg's silk screens, Warhol's multiple-image paintings, photo-realism, Larry Rivers' erasures and pseudo-pageantry, Sherrie Levine's photographs of "classic" photographs; Disneyland, Las Vegas, suburban strips, shopping malls, mirror-glass building facades; William Burroughs, Tom Wolfe, Donald Barthelme, Monty Python, Don DeLillo, Joe Isuzu "He's lying" commercials, Philip Glass, *Star Wars*, Spalding Gray, David Hockney ("Surface is illusion, but so is depth"), Max Headroom, David Byrne, Twyla Tharp (choreographic Beach Boys and Frank Sinatra songs), Italo Calvino, *The Gospel at Colonus,* Robert Wilson, the Flying Karamazov Brothers, George Coates, the Kronos Quartet, Frederick Barthelme, MTV, *Miami Vice.* . . .

Todd Gitlin, "Postmodernism Defined, At Last!" (52–53).

chapter **eighteen**

Sex had become glandular and biological... It was just naked bodies rubbing together.

When she got home, Myra Prail made an emergency call

to her therapist. She talked about Ettore Gnocchi's death for the better part of an hour. Then, just before she ended her call, she happened to mention to her therapist, Dr. Silberman, that she was involved in a postmodern experiment—creating fantasies to improve her sex life.

"I've got bored with ordinary sex," she announced, "so my lover and I decided to increase our fantasy life to improve our sex. After all, postmodernism is characterized, all the important theorists tell us, by stylistic promiscuity. I decided to reverse things and make my promiscuity stylistic! Or perhaps *stylish* would be more accurate.

"One of the more important postmodern theorists, a French scholar named Lyotard, wrote in his book *The Postmodern Condition* that, as he put it, 'eclecticism is the degree zero of contemporary culture. One listens to reggae, watches a western, eats McDonald's food for lunch and local cuisine for dinner. . . .' And he added a number of other things to his discussion of eclecticism and postmodernism. It was this matter of different foods that made me start thinking about how people in different cultures live, eat . . . and then, my breakthrough idea, Dr. Silberman, to have sex."

"Yes?" the therapist murmured.

"And that variety is the spice of postmodern life, too . . . so I thought it's variety I need. Not in terms of different lovers, since I'm fond of my present lover, but in terms of different national styles of making love. Also, it would give my lover new identities, each time, to make the relationship more interesting. It's quite wonderful having the same lover appear in different incarnations, so to speak. Variety, I thought, would improve my sex life."

"Is that so?" replied Dr. Silberman.

"Sex had become glandular and biological, if you know what I mean. It was just naked bodies rubbing together, it seemed, and I was not getting too much pleasure out of it. Just taking care of needs we had . . . it was almost clinical. He stuck this big, throbbing, reddish cucumber-like penis of his into me and we wiggled around and grunted and groaned. He always came and sometimes I did. . . . How boring . . . if you know what I mean."

"So?"

"So my lover and I decided to create fantastic scenarios to enhance our sexual lives. I hit upon the notion of staging little dramas involving what you might called ethnic and nationality stereotyping and sex. I had, for a long time, got by with fantasies that my sexual partner was an English lord with a grand house who had come riding up on a great white stallion. If I closed my eyes I could fantasize this, but it didn't work very well after a while. So I hit on the ethnic and nationality sexual-fantasies idea . . . to give our intercourse a bit of excitement and an international flavor."

"How does that work?" asked Dr. Silberman.

"Three weeks ago, for example, we did French sex. I dressed in fishnet stockings and wore high heels and a micromini, like a French streetwalker. I also wore a scarf from Hermes and Fidji perfume. My lover wore a beret and grew a pencil-thin mustache. I put French travel posters on the wall. I started things off with a French dinner."

"A French dinner?"

"Yes. We began with caviar on toast and a bottle of Moet Chandon '78. I had made vichyssoise, which I served cold with sour cream instead of chives. That was followed by a cassoulet, full of roast duck, which I served with a good Bordeaux, Lafite Rothschild '49. Then came a salad of mixed greens with vinaigrette dressing. After that, I had a lovely pear tart. Then came the cheese plate, after which we sipped Grand Marnier."

"Sounds like a lovely evening, even *without* the sex," murmured the therapist.

"Then, while we listened to songs sung by Edith Piaf, I surrendered to Jean-Baptiste—that's the name I gave him—whispering sweet nothings in his ear in French. He called me Nathalie. The next morning we had café au lait and brioche and read *Le Monde*. It was wonderful. Then we parted. He said to me, in the best French tradition, that he had to get back to his wife."

"Hmm," said Dr. Silberman. "What other nationalities did you use to have sex?"

"Two weeks ago it was Germany. I was Lola and wore a leather miniskirt and Karl-Heinz, my boyfriend, wore lederhosen, a Tyrolean hat, and leather boots. I got posters from Germany and tacked them on the walls. Then I served a nice German dinner while we listened to songs, sung in German, by Marlene Dietrich."

"How interesting."

"I started with a chopped herring, beets, and onion salad, which we had with schnapps. Then I served grilled bratwurst, red cabbage, and roast potatoes, and big steins of dark Beck's beer. We had dark pumpernickel bread, also, and we had gurkensalat—cucumber in vinegar and sugar—on the side. And, of course, a hearty mustard with horseradish in it. For dessert I served apple strudel and coffee mit schlag. Then, as Wagner's *Die Meistersinger* played on the stereo, Karl-Heinz had me—on the dining room table, no less."

"Sounds quite uncomfortable."

"Teutonic passion. Karl-Heinz couldn't wait . . . it was really quite fabulous."

"And then . . ."

"The next morning we had orange juice, coffee and hot milk, and meusli with bananas, while we read the *Berliner Zeitung*."

"Quite incredible."

"Last week we did a Jewish scenario. Menachem Mendel, which is the name my lover took, got a beard from a theater costume shop and went to the Jewish section where he bought a streimel, tsitsis, and a long black coat. I chose to call myself Rebecca. I visited a mikvah the night before to cleanse myself physically as well as spiritually, which, so I understand, is what you're supposed to do. I wore a wig, making it look as if I had dark brown hair."

"And what did you eat?"

"First we said a couple of blessings—bruchas, as they're called. You'd know that, of course, Dr. Silberman, wouldn't you? As we ate, we listened to songs sung by Schlomo Carslbach and then klezmer bands. I started our dinner off with a big bowl of chicken soup and matzoh balls . . . or kneidlach, as they're called in Yiddish. This was followed by a plate of chopped chicken livers with real shmultz and also some sweet and sour mackerel. Then we had some homemade gefilte fish, with horseradish I had grated, sliced cucumbers, and tomatoes. I had bought a large braided challah at the local Jewish bakery, which was very delicious. The main course was roast brisket—glat kosher, of course—with boiled potatoes and green peas. The wine was Manishevitz Concord . . . just like in the old days, before Jews became wine snobs like WASPs. Then we had a salad of wedges of iceberg lettuce and a mustard and vinaigrette dressing. For dessert we had honey cake and mandelbrot, and drank

Swee-Touch-Nee tea. Then we prayed some more. We ended by singing the 'Birkat Ha Mazon.' "

"Sounds like a lot of work."

"Nobody ever said being a Jew was easy. In keeping with the Jewish tradition, Menachem Mendel gave a short lecture, a 'drosh,' on the Torah, discussing the different interpretations that various rabbis had made, over the last five thousand years, of a particular passage, 'The voice is the voice of Jacob, but the hands are the hands of Esau.' Then I tossed my wig at him and we went to bed. He said a prayer for good sex and then we screwed while a CD of Israeli songs played on the stereo. After we finished, Menachem Mendel and I said some prayers thanking G-d for having had good sex. Then he gave another drosh, for half an hour, on some obscure portion of the Torah, and we fell asleep."

"Sounds *very* heady."

"It was. The next morning we had orange juice, bagels with lox and cream cheese, coffee, and Danish pastry, as we read the *Jerusalem Post*."

"And what are you planning for next weekend?" asked Dr. Silberman.

"I haven't figured that out yet. I'm kind of torn between a Turkish seraglio scenario, one with a Russian cossack . . . or something Fellini-esque with an Italian. If we do the Italian one, my lover will be called Massimo and I'll call myself Cipriana. I like those names. We'll drink a bottle of Neblida '76, which I favor very much, and screw to *La Traviata,* one of my favorite operas. I've thought of a Japanese Zen screwing, too . . . but we don't have the right kind of bathtub for that. I've got to think about it more. . . ."

Postmodernization of culture is best understood as an extension and intensification of differentiation, rationalization and commodification which dissolves the regional stability of modern culture and reverses its priorities.

Value-spheres become hyperdifferentiated, that is, their internal boundaries multiply to the point of fragmentation. As the particular genre, or style, becomes the unit of production and consumption, we orient ourselves to nostalgic classicism rather than "Art," to heavy metal rather than "Music" or to nineteenth-century women novelists rather than "Literature." The eventual effect of hyperdifferentiation is to set loose cultural "fragments" of intense symbolic power which transgresses the boundaries between value-spheres and between culture and other subsystems.

Stephen Crook, Jan Pakulski, and Malcolm Waters, *Postmodernization: Change in Advanced Society* (36).

chapter **nineteen**

My life is hair, my hair is life.
My life is hair, my hair is life.

Miyako Fuji poured herself a beer

(she chose a Kirin from her vast collection) and sat down in front of her television set. "Ettore's dead," she thought. "I really hated him . . . but his death—it was so gruesome. Others must have hated him, also . . . or so it would seem. Enough to want to kill him. I can understand that. He was a monster. I've got to take my mind off today . . . his death and that horrible detective. . . . Maybe I'll watch the experimental film I made last year again. I can't understand why it hasn't won any awards. Probably because of the racist and sexist media establishment. Bastards. I sent it to Sundance, but they rejected it. That's because Sundance has become part of our consumer culture and no longer is interested in artistic integrity and personal vision. It neglects films like mine that explore, in the best postmodern manner, the disappearance of the boundary between art and everyday life. Sundance and all the other film festivals—except for the dear Finns in Yvaskyla, who love my work—have capitulated and become hopelessly bourgeois.

"We live, as Baudrillard has argued, as voyeurs drifting in a sea of symbols, and by exploring this matter, by attacking our need for novelty and narrative, I've created quintessentially postmodern videos and films that define our reality in our stage of late capitalism. I probe the existential experience of self at its most primitive and elemental level, like Lynch in *Blue Velvet,* Wenders in *Paris, Texas,* and Woody Allen.

"But, of course, I am a woman . . . an *Asian* woman at that, and the racism and sexism in the film world is too much for me to overcome. At this moment, anyway. But an artist in a postmodern society always must have hope, for there's no telling when the feverish eclecticism that characterizes postmodern societies will find my work in favor and I will have the 'fifteen minutes of fame' that has been allotted to me."

Miyako turned on her television set, slipped a video into her VCR, and pressed a couple of buttons. The screen flickered for a moment and then her film came on.

The screen turned light pink. In the center of the screen there was a pair of yellow lips. Underneath these lips, in big green letters, appeared the title of her film:

SO**LIPS**ISM

Underneath the title, in blue letters, was the subtitle and her name:

A Postmodernist Film by Miyako Fuji

The screen faded to black. The next scene was an extreme long shot of an island full of pine trees, a large sandy beach, and in the middle, on a ridge, a huge mansion. The sun was bright and the sky blue. The camera moved slowly in on the mansion. There was a long tracking shot as the person with the video camera entered the building, which was apparently deserted, and wandered along its empty corridors and up several flights of stairs. There were shots as the camera moved through dark, mysterious passageways until, coming from under a doorway at the end of one passage, there was some light.

The door opened and revealed a large, bright room, full of vases with lilies and in the middle, in front of a full-length mirror, under a brilliantly lit chandelier, stood Miyako Fuji herself. She was dressed in a diaphanous white gown and was brushing her hair with an ornate silver brush. She had green eye makeup on and her lips were painted green, as were her nails. A CD player in the corner was playing some Chopin waltzes. Her silky black hair reached down to her waist and Miyako brushed it, over and over again, with long, delicate strokes.

As she brushed her hair she spoke in a singsong manner, almost as if she were in a trance:

"My hair. My hair . . . my hair is life, my life is my hair. . . . My hair is my life, my life is my hair. Hair . . . hair . . . my life is my hair, my hair is my life . . . hair . . . my hair is my life, my life is my hair. . . ."

This scene went on for several minutes. The camera moved in for extreme close-ups, from time to time, of her hair, her hands, her eyes, her lips. In some shots the light reflected off her silver hairbrush and in others her hair appeared almost translucent against the brilliant light coming from the chandelier on the ceiling. There were a number of other kinds of shots taken: shots from above her, from the floor, shots that framed her in lilies. And all the while, she brushed her hair with long, delicate strokes, and swaying, as if she were in a trance, she said the same thing:

"My hair, my hair . . . my hair is my life, my life is my hair. My hair . . ."

She swayed as she brushed her hair and started breathing heavily. . . . You might even think she was having an orgasm.

Suddenly that scene ended and the screen faded to black. It opened on a different scene. She was sitting alone on the beach.

It stretched before her for miles and miles. You could hear, faintly, the sound of drummers. She was staring out at the sea. The weather had changed. The sky had turned gray, and ominous-looking black clouds were racing in toward the island. A strong wind had come up. The sea had changed and turned violent, full of whitecaps that crashed into one another. Huge waves were pounding the beach.

She sat on a tatami mat. The wind tore at her and her gown flapped noisily in the wind but she sat, serenely, staring out at the sea. She now had yellow makeup on her eyes and her finger-nails were painted a translucent purple. In front of her there was a small square box, a small rectangular box, and a larger rectangular box, all of which were tied with elaborate yellow ribbons. There was also a long, thin knife. After a few minutes, she picked up the knife and gazed at it, as if under some kind of a hypnotic spell. Its bejeweled handle glistened as it caught the light. The sound of the drums grew stronger. The wind had died down, and suddenly there was an incredible stillness.

"It is time," she said, in a low voice, little louder than a whisper, as she gazed at the knife. She placed it down, gently, on the mat. "It is time." Her face filled the screen. "It is time for the resolution of the dialectic." The camera backed away from her. She reached for the small box and picked it up. She pulled on the rib-bon and it came off. She opened the box. In it was a peach. Then she picked up the knife and started peeling the peach. When she had peeled it, she put the peelings into the square box and ate the peach, with great, juicy gulps.

"Peaches are good for the complexion," she said, licking her lips with gusto. Then she picked up the long, rectangular box and opened it. She pulled out a long, thin object that was covered in dark red tissue paper. She pulled the tissue paper aside, reveal-ing a mirror. Then she quickly opened the third box, in which was a hairbrush. "And peaches are also good for one's hair," she said, as she stood up and started brushing her long black hair once again. She started singing her mantra in a singsong voice:

"My hair . . . my hair . . . my life is my hair, my hair is my life . . . hair, hair, hair . . . my hair is my life. . . ."

She still had that almost-orgasmic look on her face, as she ran her brush through her long, silky black hair. It flowed in the breeze, almost as if it had a life of its own, as she brushed it in long, sensuous strokes.

The camera zoomed in on her. She seemed to be in a trance. Then the camera lost focus. The screen faded to black. The credits rolled by:

SOLIPSISM

A Postmodernist Film by Miyako Fuji

Literature

Does the text contain shopping lists, menus, and/or recipes? Does it contain a novel within a novel that has the same title as the novel? Does the cover feature a bunch of little geometric shapes and a quote from Robert Coover? Does it remind you of Céline, if Céline had drunk a lot of Tab? Is it easy to hate?

Movies

Does it remind you of an old movie, except it's set in a post-apocalyptic wasteland? Does it remind you of an old TV show, only it's insincere and has better production values and is longer?

Theater and Performance Art

Are there video monitors, working or not, onstage? Does it seem like a parody of something, only without jokes? Have any of the performers been signed for Susan Seidelman's next film? Is it easier than old-fashioned performance art to like, but just as easy to fall asleep during?

Bruce Handy, "A Spy Guide to Post-Modern Everything" (61).

chapter **twenty**

He said that I said that she said that? What did you say that I said? No, I didn't say what she said I said...

Slavomir Propp was bored.

And he was worried, too. "I wonder," he thought, "what that detective knows . . . and what he'll find out. Police detectives are usu-. ally stupid in the mystery stories; that's the formula. But I'm not so sure that the police are as dumb as they're supposed to be. This Hunter . . . he doesn't give much away. You don't know what to make of him. He seems to be rather dull and pedestrian, going through the motions . . . he seems to be drifting, without direction . . . almost sleepwalking—but people like that scare me. I'm sure it's part of his mode of operation. To be a cipher, to not give himself or anything else away. I dealt with people like that years ago when I was with OGPU. Sometimes they're stupid and sometimes . . . well, we'll find out . . . soon enough."

The phone rang and startled him a little. He picked up the handset.

"Oh, it's you. I'm glad you called. As a matter of fact, I was thinking of calling you."

"Yes. . . . yes . . ."

"What? He said that? What did you say?"

"He said that I said that you said that? That's not true."

"I said exactly what you said . . . believe me. What did you say?"

"And what did he say?"

"Rubbish, I tell you."

"Tell me, what do you make of the inspector? Is he a fool or a sly fox? I don't know why, but he scares me. Americans are often like that . . . you can't tell whether they are incredibly stupid and vacuous or only seem that way."

"And how are you holding up? I can understand that. Somehow we draw on inner strengths we have. I can remember, years ago, when Trubetskoy was giving me a hard time. I was the chair of a search committee looking for someone to fill a chair in linguistics at the University of Moscow. It turned out, by a remarkable coincidence, that the search committee decided that I was the best candidate for the position. 'But Prince Nikolai Sergeyevich,' I said, 'is it my fault if the search committee decided I was the best person for the job?' He looked at me with an icy stare. . . . I think he had wanted someone else nominated. He had a grim look most of the time, anyway. . . . If he'd had a better sense of humor, maybe he would have lived longer. He claimed, you know, that I stole his ideas. Absolutely ridiculous."

"What? Invited for dinner? How nice. When?"

"Yes, I can make it—unless, of course, Hunter . . . unless something happens. Who else is coming?"

"How interesting."

"It will have Russian food? How kind you are, to think of me. You'll have borsht, pelmenyi, and sour cream, chicken Kiev, and poppy seed cake for dessert . . . and lots of Stoli vodka. Sounds divine. Two desserts, you say? You want my recipe for cheesecake? You'll make one for me? That's wonderful. But you must promise *not* to give this recipe to anyone else."

"You do? Good. You have a pencil and a piece of paper? Here it is.

"Let me list the ingredients first:

two eggs

one six-ounce package of cream cheese

one heaping teaspoon of flour

six and a half tablespoons of sugar

a teaspoon of lemon juice

a teaspoon of vanilla

one and a third cups of milk

"First you mix the cream cheese with a fork until it's smooth. Then you add everything else and mix it up. It's a good idea to beat it with a hand-operated rotary beater for a couple of minutes, to make sure everything is mixed together.

"For the crust you'll need:

four tablespoons of sugar

four tablespoons of butter

one egg

one cup of flour

one-half teaspoon of baking powder

"You can mix all the crust ingredients in the baking dish you'll be using. Make sure you press the dough firmly on the bottom of the dish and around the sides. Use a round soufflé dish . . . around eight inches in diameter.

"Then you pour the cheesecake filling into the dish and bake it at 350 degrees for around forty-five minutes. Let it cool and then refrigerate it. You'll have a marvelous cake. You can double the recipe if you have a larger dish. My mouth is watering already."

"Yes. We must keep our hopes up. Who knows how this madness will be resolved. I'm optimistic."

"You're scared? Don't be. Sometimes these things work themselves out in curious ways."

"Good-bye."

The room fell silent. "Curious," Slavomir thought. "Giving that recipe made me think I was right in the middle of a postmodern novel. They always have things like shopping lists, recipes, and menus in them. I guess we postmodernists like to eat. And there's nothing wrong with that, is there?

"The only problem is that too much attention is paid in postmodern cuisine to the looks of things. With the erasure of the boundaries between art and life, food has now become an art form. But some things that look good, some works of food art, don't taste very good. Too much focus on the aesthetic and not enough on the taste.

"The aestheticization of everyday life can become absurd. I mean, give me a plate of borsht that tastes good, with a nice dollop or two of sour cream and a boiled potato. Maybe with some pumpernickel bread and a glass of vodka on the side? I don't want borsht that looks good but tastes lousy. I want beets and cabbage, sour salt, tomatoes, a rich beef broth.

"We postmodernists blur boundaries between high and low culture, between art and everyday life, and we mix up genres and styles. But food that becomes art is better to look at than eat, most of the time. It's like that new cuisine that was popular a while back. Beautiful to look at but nothing to eat."

Slavomir Propp went to his refrigerator and looked in the freezer compartment. No cake. He found a carton of Ben and Jerry's Brazilian Nut Vanilla Supremo that was half full of ice cream. He pulled out the carton, took a teaspoon from a drawer, then swapped it for a serving spoon and started wolfing down the ice cream.

The fundamental codes of a culture—those governing its language, its schemas of perception, its exchanges, its techniques, its values, the hierarchy of its practices—establish for every man, from the very first, the empirical orders with which he will be dealing and within which he will be at home. At the other extremity of thought, there are the scientific theories or the philosophical interpretations which explain why order exists in general, what universal law it obeys, what principle can account for it, and why this particular order has been established and not some other.

Michel Foucault,
The Order of
Things: An
Archaeology of
the Human
Sciences **(xx).**

chapter **twenty-one**

Let me sketch out some scenarios that might explain his death...

"Who was responsible for the death of Ettore Gnocchi?"

wondered Police Inspector Solomon Hunter, alone in his flat. "I've some ideas, but first I've got a little more checking to do."

The next morning he went into his office very early and made a number of phone calls; one of them was to Italy. Then he read the forensics report from the doctor who did the postmortem. "Very interesting," he thought. Then, Hunter drove to 5000 Pacific Street. As he had requested, everyone was there in the living room, drinking coffee and looking glum. The silence was funereal.

"Good morning," he said brightly, to throw them all off. "I'd like to resolve this case this morning. And I believe I can. I will tell you how Ettore Gnocchi died. Obviously, someone in the house that night was responsible for his death. But who?"

The people in the room looked at Hunter with frightened expressions on their faces. Nobody said anything.

"Let me sketch out some possible scenarios that might explain Ettore Gnocchi's death."

"Scenario one. I called Italy earlier and discovered that Gnocchi had an identical twin brother, one Erculeo 'Big Thumbs' Gnocchi. He was an enforcer for the Mafia and had been in prison for thirty years for killing a dozen people. He was part of a gang of thieves and killers in Palermo called 'The Philosophers,' because one member of the gang could read. His colleagues were most disreputable and infamous. His lieutenant was Rinaldo 'The Fisherman' Compesini. The other members of the gang were Tomaso 'Talking Horse' Chibiocchi, Michaelangelo 'The Rejecter' Alleni, Giordiano 'The Poet' Massimani, and Ricardo 'The Professor' Clinton-Websteri. He was the one who knew how to read.

"But Erculeo Gnocchi was just released a month ago and seems to have disappeared from sight. He may have come to America. The body we saw at the table could have been his? Maybe he died or was killed, for some reason, by Ettore? Or Erculeo could have killed his brother? When the lights went out, if this scenario is correct, the dead body of one of the Gnocchi twins was planted by the other one. It would only have taken an instant, though the body would have to have been recently killed and stored somewhere in the house. This is, I admit, really far-fetched . . . but it's something we've got to consider." Hunter paused to let the others catch up with him, for most of them looked stunned.

"Now we're ready for scenario two. Four people at the table, each acting independently, without knowing what any of the others were doing, tried to kill Gnocchi. One person shot him through the head, using a gun with a silencer. Another stabbed him in the back with a stiletto . . . the one that had been used to cut up the panettone that Propp brought." Miyako Fuji uttered a little gasp and clapped her hands to her lips, and Hunter glared at her.

"And a third person blew a poison dart into his cheek. We've checked on the poison. It's from the skin of a rare poisonous frog found only in the rain forests of Sumatra, *Rana korriganus morrealus*. And a fourth poisoned his drink. The drink that spilled on the tablecloth was analyzed and proves to have been laced with arsenic.

"Just about everyone at the table had a motive to kill Gnocchi. His wife was jealous of him and angry about his infidelities. Myra Prail, who's doing her dissertation under him—literally as well as figuratively, so it seems—felt exploited by him. Propp claims his ideas were stolen by Gnocchi, who became famous as the result of his being a plagiarist. Gnocchi almost drove Fess to suicide when Fess worked on his dissertation with him. Fuji was, it would seem, either seduced or raped by Gnocchi. The only one who doesn't have a strong motive is Constant, and I bet if we dig around a bit more we'll find he has a good motive, too." Some of the suspects looked calm, others mortified.

"Scenario three. Gnocchi, playing some kind of cosmic joke, somehow killed himself. He knew he was going to die soon because of his heart problems. So he decided to expedite matters. He shot himself after he somehow stuck the knife in his back and that dart in his cheek. The knife wound was not a fatal one and the poison takes a while to act. He must have arranged for someone to take the gun and get rid of it. We didn't find it when we searched the house. Maybe it was hidden in the panettone?"

"Are you accusing me?" asked Propp, indignantly.

"I'm not accusing anyone, for the moment," said Hunter.

"Finally," Hunter continued, "let me move on to scenario number four. Here's something most interesting. Here's what Shoshana TelAviv told me when I interrogated her. These are her exact words: 'I heard a funny noise . . . like a hiss of a snake . . . just after I heard Ettore utter a soft groan.' What she said confused me at first, because the term 'after' was ambiguous. But now I've concluded that what she meant was that Gnocchi screamed 'Aah' and *then* she heard a hissing sound—which was the sound of a gun with a silencer.

"What happened, I believe, is that Gnocchi had a sudden heart attack and was dead in an instant—seconds before all the people who were trying to murder him made their attempts to do so. I checked with his doctor and Gnocchi was in very bad shape. His doctor said that Gnocchi was living on borrowed time . . . and I noticed, when I watched a video of his last lecture at the university, that Gnocchi had to stop in the middle of his lecture to take some pills. He also mentioned, in one of his letters, which I read in his own office, that his doctor had told him not to worry. And that advice was, I would suggest, given him because he was a dead man walking, so to speak. The autopsy confirmed that he died instantly."

The silence in the room was profound, Hunter noted with grim pleasure. Finally, someone spoke. "You mean," asked Shoshana, "Ettore had died before he was shot and before he was . . ."

"Yes. In the best postmodern tradition, his would-be murderers were, ironically, attempting to kill a dead man. Which means, technically speaking, nobody actually murdered Gnocchi, even though a number of people may have attempted to do so."

"Well," asked Myra Prail, "which scenario do you think is the correct one?"

"I've been giving the matter a lot of thought. . . . I think the postmodern solution, the last one, is the *right* one. Let's say that I see no reason to lock up a number of people for attempting to kill a dead man, even if each of you, who are incredulous about meta-narratives, had what you thought was a good reason to kill Ettore Gnocchi. I'm going to give all of you the benefit of the doubt and not press charges. His death was, I think it's fair to say, exquisitely postmodern."

A postmodern artist or writer is in the position of a philosopher: the text he writes, the work he produces are not in principle governed by preestablished rules and they cannot be judged according to a determining judgment, by applying familiar categories to the text or to the work. Those rules and categories are what the work of art itself is looking for. The artist and the writer, then, are working without rules in order to formulate the rules of what *will have been done.* Hence the fact that work and text have the character of an *event*; hence also, they always come too late for their author, or, what amounts to the same thing, their being put into work, their realization (*mise en oeuvre*) always begin too soon. *Post modern* would have to be understood according to the paradox of the future: (*post*) anterior (*modo*).

Jean-François Lyotard, *The Postmodern Condition: A Report on Knowledge* (81).

chapter **twenty-two**

The next day Basil Constant started a new novel

entitled *Postmortem for a Postmodernist.* Its first chapter reads as follows:

When the lights went on again, the head of Professor Ettore Gnocchi was lying on the table. There was a small red hole, from which a thin trickle of blood was flowing, in the middle of his forehead. The handle of a silver stiletto protruded from his back, and around the stiletto the material on Gnocchi's sports jacket was stained a dark red. A long wooden dart, with yellow feathers, was lodged in his right cheek, several inches from his mouth. The glass of wine, which he had just started drinking, had spilled onto the tablecloth, from which a slightly sulfuric-smelling mist was rising.

There was, curiously, something that resembled a smile frozen on his face.

selected **bibliography**

Barthes, Roland. (1962) *Mythologies*. New York: Hill & Wang.

Baudrillard, Jean. (1968) *Le Système des Objets*. Paris: Denoel-Gonthier.

———. (1975) *The Mirror of Production*. St. Louis: Telos Press.

———. (1983) *Simulations*. New York: Semiotext(e).

———. "On Nihilism." *On the Beach* 6 (spring 1984).

———. (1988) *America*. London: Verso.

Benjamin, Andrew (ed.). (1989) *The Lyotard Reader*. Oxford, England: Basil Blackwell.

Berger, Arthur Asa. (1997a) *Bloom's Morning: Toothpaste, Toasters and the Secret Meaning of Everyday Life*. Boulder, Colo.: Westview/HarperCollins.

———. (1997b) *The Genius of the Jewish Joke*. Northvale, N.J.: Jason Aronson.

———. (1997c) *Narratives in Media, Popular Culture and Everyday Life*. Thousand Oaks, Calif.: Sage Publications.

———. (1997d) *The Art of Comedy Writing*. New Brunswick, N.J.: Transaction Publishers.

Berman, Marshall. (1982) *All That Is Solid Melts into Air: The Experience of Modernity*. London: Verso.

Best, Steven, and Douglas Kellner. (1991) *Postmodern Theory: Critical Interrogations*. New York: The Guilford Press.

Connor, Steve. (1989) *Postmodernist Culture.* Oxford, England: Basil Blackwell.

Constant, Basil. (1981) *Constrictor.* London: Spotted Dick Press.

———. **(1985) *Chameleon.* London: Spotted Dick Press.**

Crook, Stephen, Jan Pakulski, and Malcolm Waters (eds.). (1992) *Postmodernization: Change in Advanced Society.* London: Sage Publications.

DeBord, Guy. (1970) *Society of the Spectacle.* Detroit: Black and Red.

Deleuze, Giles. (1986) *Foucault.* Minneapolis: University of Minnesota Press.

Denzin, Norman K. (1991) *Images of Postmodern Society: Social Theory and Contemporary Cinema.* London: Sage Publications.

Featherstone, Mike. (1991) *Consumer Culture and Postmodernism.* London: Sage Publications.

———. (ed.). (1988) *Theory, Culture and Society: Special Issue on Postmodernism.* London: Sage Publications.

Fess, Alain. (1986) *Minotaur: The Beast in the Shopping Mall.* (Trans. Jean-Marie de Benoist.) Paris: Nul Presse.

Foster, Hal (ed.). (1983) *The Anti-Aesthetic: Essays on Postmodern Culture.* Port Townsend, Wash.: Bay Press.

Foucault, Michel. (1973a) *Madness and Civilization: A History of Insanity in the Age of Reason.* New York: Vintage Books.

———. (1973b) *The Order of Things: An Archaeology of the Human Sciences.* New York: Vintage Books.

———. (1979) *Discipline and Punish.* New York: Vintage Press.

Fuji, Miyako. *Screenplay for "Solipsism."* Hollywood, Calif.: Narcissus Press.

Gitlin, Todd. (1989) "Postmodernism Defined, At Last!" *Dissent* (winter 1989). Quoted in *Utne Reader* 30 (May/June 1989).

Gottdiener, Mark. (1995) *Postmodern Semiotics: Material Culture and the Forms of Postmodern Life.* Oxford, England: Basil Blackwell.

Gnocchi, Ettore. (1985) *The Postmodern Prisoner.* Cambridge, Mass.: Harvard University Press.

Habermas, Jürgen. (1976) *Communication and the Evolution of Society.* Boston: Beacon Press.

———. (1989) *The Structural Transformation of the Public Sphere.* Cambridge, Mass.: MIT Press.

Handy, Bruce (1988) "A Spy Guide to Postmodern Everything." *Spy Magazine* (April 1988).

Harvey, David. (1989) *The Condition of Postmodernity.* Oxford, England: Basil Blackwell.

Hebdige, Dick. (1988) *Hiding in the Light: On Images and Things.* London: Routledge.

Hollinger, Robert. (1994) *Postmodernism and the Social Sciences.* Thousand Oaks, Calif.: Sage Publications.

Hutcheon, Linda. (1990) *A Poetics of Postmodernism: History, Theory, Fiction.* New York and London: Routledge.

Jameson, Fredric. (1983) "Postmodernism and Consumer Society." In H. Foster (ed.), *The Anti-Aesthetic: Essays on Postmodern Culture.* Port Townsend, Wash.: Bay Press.

———. (1991) *Postmodernism, or The Cultural Logic of Late Capitalism.* Durham, N.C.: Duke University Press.

Jencks, Charles. (1977) *The Language of Post-Modern Architecture.* New York: Rizzoli.

Kellner, Douglas. (1988) "Postmodernism as Social Theory: Some Challenges and Problems." *Theory, Culture and Society* 5:2–3 (June 1988).

———. (1989) *Jean Baudrillard: From Marxism to Postmodernism and Beyond.* Stanford, Calif.: Stanford University Press.

———. (1990) *Television and the Crisis of Democracy.* Boulder, Colo.: Westview Press.

Kroker, Arthur, and David Cook. (1986) *The Postmodern Scene: Excremental Culture and Hyper-Aesthetics.* New York: St. Martin's Press.

Kvale, Steinar. (1992) "Postmodern Psychology: A Contradiction in Terms?" In Steinar Kvale (ed.), *Psychology and Postmodernism.* London: Sage Publications.

Lyotard, Jean-François. (1984) *The Postmodern Condition: A Report on Knowledge*. Minneapolis: University of Minnesota Press.

Navarro, Desiderio (ed.). "Postmodernism: Center and Periphery." *South Atlantic Quarterly* 92:3 (summer 1993).

Poster, Mark. (1975) *Existential Marxism in Postwar France*. Princeton, N.J.: Princeton University Press.

———. (1990) *Mode of Information*. Cambridge, Mass.: Polity Press.

Propp, Slavomir. (1992) *Morphology of Modernism*. Moscow: Yistvostyik Press.

Ross, Andrew. (1989) *No Respect: Intellectuals and Popular Culture*. New York: Routledge.

———. (ed.) (1988) *Universal Abandon: The Politics of Postmodernism*. Minneapolis: University of Minnesota Press.

Simons, Herbert S., and Michael Billig (eds.). (1994) *After Postmodernism: Reconstructing Ideology Critique*. London: Sage Publications.

Turner, Bryan S. (ed.). (1990) *Theories of Modernity and Postmodernity*. London: Sage Publications.

NOTE: Books by fictional characters in the book are in **bold** print.

names **index**

about the **author**

Arthur Asa Berger, an improper Bostonian, is a writer, artist, and self-appointed secret agent. He took his B.A. in Literature at the University of Massachusetts in Amherst in 1954 and received an M.A. in Journalism from the University of Iowa in 1956. He was the music, art, and theater critic for the *Daily Iowan*—that is, "the cultural commissar of Iowa City." Two weeks after graduation he was drafted into the U.S. Army (he is a trained killer) and served in Washington, D.C., where he worked in the public information office of the Military District of Washington until 1958. He also wrote sports pieces for the *Washington Post* on weekend evenings during this period.

Berger received his Ph.D. in American Studies from the University of Minnesota in Minneapolis in 1965. His dissertation was on Li'l Abner and American satire. He has taught at San Francisco State University from 1965 to the present. (He will be retiring from San Francisco State University in January of 1998 and thus will be available for lectures, seminars, short courses, and light catering.) Berger has published more than thirty books on media, popular culture, humor, and related concerns. *Postmortem for a Postmodernist* is Berger's first work of fiction, though many critics argue that all his books and articles should be thought of as fiction.

He is married to a philosophy professor and has two children, "my son, the mathematician" and "my daughter, the actress." He lives in Mill Valley, California.

His Internet address is *aberger@sfsu.edu*. He can also be reached by snail mail at the Broadcast & Electronic Communication Arts Department at San Francisco State University.